Contents

Part 2 Finding the Right Manufacturer for Your House

FIFTH EDITION

MANUFACTURED HOUSES

Finding and Buying Your Dream Home for Less

A. M. WATKINS

DEARBORN™
A **Kaplan Professional** Company

Associate Publisher: Cynthia A. Zigmund
Senior Managing Editor: Jack Kiburz
Interior Design: Elizandro Carrington
Cover Design: Jill Shimabukuro
Cover Photos: Top photo: Chesterfield House by AvisAmerica.
© AvisAmerica. For more information, call 1-800-AvisAmerica.
Middle photo: Bayshore A House by AvisAmerica. © AvisAmerica.
Bottom photo: Caretakers Cottage by Haven Homes, Inc. © Michael Mundy. Reprinted with permission.

Library of Congress Cataloging-in-Publication Data
Watkins, A.M. (Arthur Martin), 1924 –
    Manufactured houses : finding and buying your dream home
for less   /   A.M. Watkins.—5th ed.
        p.   cm.
    Rev. ed. of: The complete guide to factory-made houses.
Newly rev. 1988.
    Includes index.
    ISBN 0-7931-1149-8
    1. House buying.   2. Prefabricated houses—Purchasing.
I. Watkins, A.M. (Arthur Martin), 1924 –   Complete guide to
factory-made houses.   II. Title.
HD1379.W343   1994   94-13201
693'.97—dc20   CIP

Dearborn books are available at special quantity discounts to use as premiums and sales promotions, or for use in corporate training programs. For more information, please call the Special Sales Manager at 800-621-9621, ext. 4514, or write to Dearborn Financial Publishing, Inc., 155 N. Wacker Drive, Chicago, IL 60606-1719.

Books by A.M. Watkins

How To Avoid the Ten Biggest Homebuying Traps
The Homeowner's Survival Kit
Dollars and Sense
Buying Land: How To Profit from the Last Great Land Boom
The New Complete Book of Home Remodeling,
Improvement, & Repair
Building and Buying the High-Quality House at Lowest Cost

Preface

Anyone who builds or buys a new house today without looking into the new manufactured houses now available could be passing up the opportunity of a lifetime. It's like buying a foreign car without looking into the new models offered by Detroit manufacturers—or vice versa. Except that a house involves a higher level of commitment.

You'll never know what you might have missed, including a bigger and better house with handsome styling, often significant money savings, as well as other potential benefits. It's like the family that feeds on meat and potatoes before discovering other dishes such as Italian pasta, not to mention French and Chinese food.

Factory house manufacturers offer better design and construction than most conventionally built houses. They offer houses in every style, size and price range, savings in time and money and unique opportunities and options when you build or buy a factory-made house. Are they here to stay? Absolutely yes. Houses made in whole or in part in factories now account for as much as 40 percent or more of all new houses in the United States. In short, the manufactured house has arrived in the United States, just as it has in other countries such as Sweden, Denmark and, not surprisingly, Japan.

This book is your guide to all kinds of manufactured houses in the United States. The goal of this book is to tell you all about building or buying a manufactured house so that you too can take advantage of this opportunity. Accompanying photographs show examples of this new breed of house, one of which could be just the house you've always wanted for you and your family.

Note: We advise that you use this book only as a general aid. Before building or buying a house, consult the appropriate professionals familiar with such a house design and construction.

▲ PART 1 ▲
How To Buy a Manufactured House

A Better Mousetrap: The New Manufactured House

A well-known national magazine recently published a special report on manufactured homes in the United States. It was peppered with photos of the factory-made houses being sold today nationwide. If these houses were not identified as factory-made, few people would have recognized the houses for what they are. I'd bet my mortgage on it.

Many homebuyers, unaware of the revolution going on in the prefab business, would never guess that these impressive houses were built in factories. In fact, take a look at the houses on the front cover. Would you have guessed that any of these three were manufactured?

But that's only part of the story. When the magazine hit the newsstands, the manufacturer of one of the houses in the report was swamped with a "thousand" calls and queries about it from around the country. He was stunned.

Since it was first made in America some 60 years ago, the manufactured house has clearly come of age. It's no longer a baby. In the early 1930s, Sears Roebuck offered a prefab house in its catalog. Even before then, visionary architects like Frank

Lloyd Wright drew plans for houses made in factories that would cut housing costs for people who couldn't afford *stickbuilt* (conventionally made) houses.

Recently, *The New York Times* Sunday magazine published a story about a "modest" prefab that had been put up in the luxury suburb of Greenwich, Connecticut (see Figure 1.1). The *Times* writer said, "The house arrived in pieces on the back of a truck. Two days later, it was standing erect. . . . None of its neighbors would have guessed [it] was a prefab."

But what a prefab! It may be modest in that fancy suburb, but its handsome architectural design would rate four stars virtually anywhere in the country. Few professional architects could fault its architecture. Its construction specifications make a statement: The house conforms to the Connecticut building code, one of the toughest codes in the nation. That should give it acceptance in virtually every state.

Many home manufacturers will also prefabricate houses for a buyer from the buyer's plans or specification. Actually, you don't need formal plans. A simple sketch showing the kind of plan you want is often enough. The manufacturer takes it from there, drawing up plans for your approval, and then makes the house. That's how to get a custom house at an affordable price.

A number of manufacturers offer top-quality design and construction. Some make stunning houses, as the photographs in this book show. However, just as the quality of conventional stickbuilt houses can vary, the design and quality of some factory-made houses can vary too. Nonetheless, because of technology and the quality control possible under a roof and on an assembly line, the quality of manufactured houses generally stands head and shoulders over that of stickbuilt houses.

A *manufactured house*, also called a *factory-made house*, is a house that is built in whole or in large part in a roof-covered factory and shipped to the site where it will be erected. In short, the house is *prefabricated*. The degree of prefabrication (prefab) varies according to type and manufacturer. The four main types of manufactured houses are described in detail in this book.

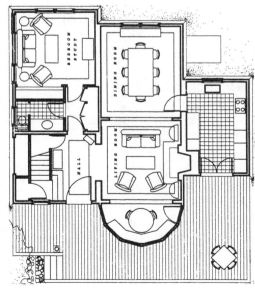

Figure 1.1 *This modular house, also shown on the front cover, was delivered by truck to its Connecticut site in five sections, which were erected in two days, three side by side and two on top. Local workers provided the finishing touches. Caretakers Cottage manufactured by Haven Homes, Inc. Floor plan used with permission by Ike & Kligerman Architects. Photo © Michael Mundy. Reprinted with permission.*

■ HOW MUCH CAN YOU SAVE ■
ON A FACTORY-MADE HOUSE?

The amount of money you can save depends on the size and type of house you want and how much do-it-yourself work you can provide. To start with, there may be little or no apparent dollar savings on a custom house bought from a home manufacturer, especially when the house is completely erected and finished for you, with little or no work provided by you.

The dollar cost of such a house generally will be about the same as it would cost to build the same house conventionally. However, the factory-made version of the house will usually be better designed and better built. It will be subject to fewer construction problems, delays and cost overruns, and often it can be built twice as fast. These benefits can translate into significant dollar savings.

Savings can run as high as 30 percent, sometimes more, if you provide at least a good part of the labor to build your own kit house, as well as serving as your own contractor. But building a house is by no means easy. It usually requires all the help you can get from friends and relatives, as well as muscles you never knew you had. There's also a limit to the savings one can make by building a house, factory or stickbuilt. That's because construction labor accounts for only about 16 to 20 percent of the cost of an average house, according to The National Association of Home Builders (NAHB).

If you buy a modular house, one of the four main kinds of factory houses, you might save only about 10 percent, more or less, compared to buying a locally built stick house of comparable size and type. The modular house is virtually complete when it leaves the factory. It is the ultimate manufactured house, shipped in one or more sections that on delivery are lifted onto a foundation, its permanent location, and connected together. A minimum of completion work is required to make the house ready for occupancy. Since very little labor remains to complete the work on site, you won't save very much by completing it yourself. Modular houses are discussed in greater detail in Chapter 4.

Figure 1.2 *Manufactured houses offer style and design that can be tailor-made for virtually any site and location. This makes for comfortable living, to put it mildly. Deck House, Inc., Acton, MA.*

■ WIDE RANGE OF MANUFACTURERS AND ■
CHOICES FOR BUYERS

Factory-made houses are available in every size, type and style, and for every homebuyer. Not including mobile homes, about 300 to 350 home manufacturers are located in nearly every part of the country. Nobody knows the exact number.

Also, an unknown number of home manufacturers specialize in selling factory-made houses just for builders or homebuyers in a limited radius of their small plant location. Some are basically lumberyards that also specialize in providing prefabricated structural parts for builder houses.

Other manufacturers are former home builders who got wise. Now they can operate under a roof year-round in their own small plants. They are no longer slaves to the weather and outside elements. This means no more unpredictable construction delays and other higher costs. Some manufacturers in small towns or rural areas turn out 20 to 25 houses a year, others 40 to 50 a year or more.

Until a few years ago, houses made in home factories accounted for a small number of all new U.S. houses built each year. Now they are streaming out of factories, and houses made in whole or in part in factories account for as much as 40 percent of all new houses in the United States! This bodes well for nearly everyone who plans to build or buy a new house.

A factory house also can be bought from a local builder or factory dealer who specializes in putting up one or more factory houses at a time. Some sell a specific manufacturer's houses and will, if desired, modify any model for you. Others build on speculation, putting up factory houses one after the other and then placing a "For Sale" sign on each. In fact, a growing number of home builders, from the smallest- to largest-volume ones, are switching to factory houses made for them by manufacturers. See Part 2 for a directory of home manufacturers.

■   A WIDE RANGE OF PRICES   ■

At the low end, prices start at about $25,000 for complete houses, though obviously not big ones. That little money will get a buyer a compact one-bedroom mobile home adequate for a small family. Most mobile homes come furnished, including kitchen appliances, wall-to-wall carpeting, and a mattress and double bed in the rear. All you need to move in is food for the refrigerator and dishes for the kitchen table.

In addition to mobile homes, there are significant other breeds of factory houses. These fall largely in the $50,000 to

First Floor   *Second Floor*

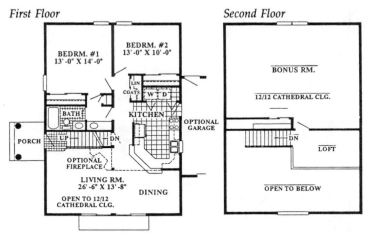

Figure 1.3 *This compact Cape Cod house offers you 1,100 square feet on the first floor, plus 464 square feet on the second floor, a total of 1,564 total square feet of living area. The living room has a cathedral ceiling under its steep roof, plus four glass doors that open up the house to the outdoor living area. Bayshore A house and floor plan reprinted with permission by AvisAmerica. © AvisAmerica.*

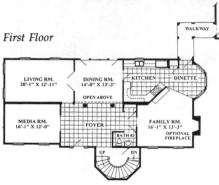

First Floor

Second Floor

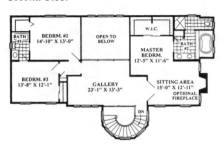

Figure 1.4 *This large "French Eclectic" house has 3,350 square feet of living area and, among other things, a circular staircase for navigating your way to the top of the turret. Chesterfield house and floor plan reprinted with permission by AvisAmerica.* © *AvisAmerica.*

$250,000 price range, the same bell curve concentration found in the conventional new-house market, though prices are continually being pushed up by inflation. A growing number of higher-priced models are also available.

The higher-priced luxury houses include custom-made models. They usually start with a maker's basic plan that is modified in a factory in various ways for different homebuyers. Very large and expensive houses are also sold, including models sold for more than $500,000. New England Components/Techbuilt reportedly made the first million-dollar factory house for a Massachusetts family in 1978, though it's not clear how much of that price is accounted for by the cost of the land.

The new factory houses fit naturally into residential America because many are absolutely indistinguishable from conventional site-built homes. Some owners don't even know that they are living in a manufactured house! For example, a well-heeled Ohio man who had bought and moved into a large two-year-old house complained about prefabricated houses, a naughty word, that were planned for a nearby tract of new houses. A neighbor gently told the complainer that he lived in a prefabricated factory house, albeit a large, expensive model. "All the houses in this development, in fact, are manufactured houses," he was told.

■ **THE ACID TEST** ■

More and more homebuilders have not only accepted manufactured houses, but a growing number are using them in developments in the $100,000-and-up house market. Some builders shop for factory houses that are already available and that they like. What's more, manufacturers can not only offer new houses in a wide range of sizes, but they can also offer savings to homebuyers.

Other builders bring their plans to manufacturers who, in turn, make builders' houses to order in their factory. Builders can

Figure 1.5 *You'd never guess the kind of finished house that is being prefabbed by walking through the factory where it was built, or if you happened by when each section of the house rolled down steel runners onto a waiting truck for delivery. Unibilt Industries, Inc. Reprinted with permission.*

have their cake and eat it, too. They put up the same kinds of houses, in design and looks, as they would ordinarily put up themselves, and they enjoy the benefits, economies and speed that are made possible by factory production.

Many manufacturers also make custom-made factory houses for individuals. People bring their plans, including houses designed for them by architects, to manufacturers who will turn out all the pieces and parts for the house. These are then assembled quickly at the site. Houses made in factories have become more widely accepted in a growing number of localities in the United States.

Perhaps all around the world, too. Foreigners, particularly in the developing countries, are ordering factory houses from U.S. manufacturers (and also from Europe), even though they must pay a stiff extra price of 20 percent or more for overseas shipping charges to their countries. Foreign buyers are continually requesting bids on factory houses from manufacturers. One U.S. manufacturer, Marvin Schuette, president of Wausau Homes, told me that at the time he had some $100 million worth of bids for his houses out for consideration by foreign governments that came to Wausau in need of housing. Manufactured houses have not only passed the acid test of homebuilder approval, but picky architects and skeptical foreigners have also become believers as well.

The idea of making homes in a factory and shipping them to the point of use is by no means new. The first prefabricated house in the new world was made in England about 1670 and shipped to Cape Ann in Massachusetts. Others followed, including a number sent to early Cape Cod settlers. More than 500 prefabricated houses were shipped to California from New York during the 1849 Gold Rush; more were shipped there from Europe and from China. In the 1890s, at least two U.S. manufacturers were turning out prefabricated houses on a paying basis; one of them, Hodgson Houses, was still in business in New England until recently.

■ Four Main Kinds of ■ Manufactured Houses

There are four types of manufactured houses (Chapters 4–8 describe them in more detail): modular (also called sectional), panelized, precut and the mobile home. The first three differ in degree of completion of the house package when it leaves the factory. The *modular* is the most complete, a three-dimensional house 95 percent complete when it comes off the assembly line. (See Figure 1.5.) It is shipped in two or more sections for set-down at the site. There it is hooked up to water, electricity and other utility lines required to light the house and make the appliances work. Then you can move right in and begin enjoying your new home.

Panelized and *precut* houses are made in two successively reduced stages of factory completion. Each thus requires respectively more completion work at the site. Fourth is the well-known mobile home. New versions of it being introduced are low in cost and attractive in design. There are also log cabin, dome and A-frame houses. The last three categories, however, have to do with the type, style and architectural design, rather than the method and extent of factory production.

Some manufacturers of factory houses other than mobile homes do not, by the way, accept the mobile home as a

Figure 1.6 *Last of four sections of this structure is lowered into place to complete the delivery of the house. Sections are sealed and bolted together, finishing touches are completed and the house can be ready for occupancy in a matter of days. Nanticoke Homes. Reprinted with permission.*

"manufactured" house. They acknowledge only three major forms of factory-made houses: modular, panelized and precut. This relegates the mobile home, by implication, to an inferior category of house. Yet by *Webster's* definition, a mobile home is not only made in a factory; it is also more completely made there than any other kind of manufactured home. It is 100 percent factory made, a manufactured house by definition. Some mobile homes are reasonably attractive; they are being anchored to permanent foundations and are financed and taxed in the same way as conventional houses. There are four breeds of manufactured houses, and this book describes each.

More significantly, it is clear that houses today finally are being made logically. Buying anything else but a factory house could soon become as old-fashioned and obsolete as buying a house without running water.

That's no big surprise. As mentioned earlier, this was predicted by eminent architects, including Frank Lloyd Wright and Walter Gropius, a leader of the celebrated Bauhaus movement in Germany some 70 years ago. Each believed in the cause of factory-built houses and designed pioneering houses for mass production in house factories. Amen.

Saving Money with a Manufactured House

Often, you can save a good deal of money on a new factory-made house simply by ordering a manufacturer's standard house from his or her catalog. This may discourage many people, since it implies purchasing a standard, mass-produced product, like the same car that many other people also have.

But it need not be that bad. For one thing, lots of people have Cadillacs and BMWs. For another, many stock model factory houses are attractive, well-made structures that offer financial savings, compared with buying or building a custom house.

■ HOW MUCH CAN YOU SAVE? ■

How much can you save? This is hard to pin down. The savings vary greatly according to the type and brand of house and where it's sold. Two major savings made with factory houses result from their high-quality construction and the speed of completion. These can mean significant money savings for reasons cited in Chapter 3.

The actual dollars saved on the purchase price of a factory house may range from nothing at all for some to a great deal, according to different sources. A spokesperson for the Building Systems Council of the National Association of Home Builders says that, excluding mobile homes, the savings "average about 5 to 10 percent." Other sources say that they can go up to 30 percent, more or less. The largest savings of all are made with mobile homes, where the savings average nearly 50 percent, as shown in Chapter 8.

■   WHERE TO DISCOVER SAVINGS   ■

Your potential savings can vary depending on a number of factors. Understanding what they are can shed light on factory houses and show you how to save the most when you buy a particular manufactured home.

House Quality

First, consider house quality. Good-quality construction costs more. One manufacturer says that this means reduced savings for this reason: "Take all the 2 × 4 wall studs used in our houses. They're Number One grade, and recently they cost us $1.25 apiece. Local builders in this area, our competition, use utility grade 2 × 4s at a cost as low as 69¢ each. That's a big difference. We pay up to twice as much for good lumber. It really adds up when you consider the hundreds of studs that go into the walls of a house.

"Now take into account the extra cost for the extra quality that goes into the other materials in a house. That's no small potatoes, since some 10 to 15 tons of building materials go into a house. That's a significant extra cost item for the factory house. It offsets some of the savings made as a result

Figure 2.1 *Traditional colonial house has the red brick exterior and attic dormers of a Jefferson house. No need to show it's standard floor plan: center hall, kitchen and dining room on one side and living room on the other. This house, a manufacturer's model, appropriately is made in Virginia. Photo courtesy of Nationwide Homes.*

of factory houses being made faster and more efficiently than stickbuilt houses.''

It may also be true that some good builders also use top-notch Number One lumber in their stickbuilt houses, as is claimed. But then their house prices will also be higher than the usual locally built builder house. Comparing these better-made stickbuilt houses with equivalent factory-made houses is now comparing apples with apples. In this case, the factory-made house will almost always be the low-cost winner, since it can be made faster, more efficiently and at lower cost in the factory.

Degree of Completion and On-site Labor Costs

Savings will also vary according to the degree of completion of the house when it leaves the factory. Because mobile homes and modular houses are virtually fully made in the factory, they require the least high-cost, on-site labor after delivery. Modular and sectional houses—about 95 percent complete on delivery— offer the next greatest savings.

You will save progressively less money with a panelized house and least of all, with one exception, when you buy a precut house. The precut is the skinniest factory package and therefore requires the most on-site completion work. The exception is building your own precut house and thereby saving a lot as your reward for using your own labor and elbow grease.

Custom Changes

Asking Ford or General Motors to stop its assembly line to make custom changes on the new car you ordered would cost a small fortune. The cost of your car, stopped in effect in mid-air while it's being modified, would not only go up sharply, but the cost of delays with the other cars on the line would also rise.

In similar fashion, asking a home manufacturer to make changes in one of his or her standard houses can also cost extra money. These changes might include adding a room or another closet or two. Whatever, they mean stop-and-go interruption with the production flow of houses being made. Changes requested might also require special plans to be prepared by the architectural department, and other people in the plant must also change gears to accommodate the changes. Figure 2.2 shows a custom manufactured house.

Unlike high-volume Detroit assembly lines, house factories can make custom changes in their houses to suit homebuyers. The factory production of houses is still in its infancy, and most house assembly lines operate at comparatively slow speed. Nonetheless, custom changes cost extra money and hence reduce factory houses savings. For that matter, asking a local builder to make custom changes in one of his or her houses will also mean a

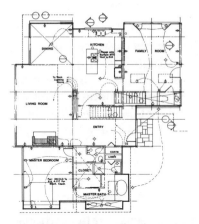

Figure 2.2 *Contemporary house exemplifies the handsome custom design, the high quality of custom houses available from home manufacturers and, among other things, what you can get from a manufacturer who uses top-quality architects. Deck House, Inc., Acton, MA.*

higher price for the house. Moral: Keep your custom changes to a minimum. Shop for a maker's model that is suitable for you with few or no changes.

Delivery Costs

Delivery costs eat into savings. The longer the distance a house is shipped from plant to site, obviously the higher its shipping cost. In one way or another, the buyer pays this cost. The maximum distance that manufacturers generally ship is about 500 miles, and many limit their deliveries to shorter distances. Because there is no standard shipping distance, delivery costs vary from buyer to buyer.

Dealer Markup

Markup is another variable that, like a seesaw, affects house prices. The more a builder-dealer marks up the sales price, obviously the less the buyer saves. Some makers put firm prices on their houses, and builder-dealers must toe the line on these prices. The retail prices on other manufacturers' houses are, for various reasons, set by the local builder-dealer. As a result, a builder in one area may charge more for a particular house than another builder in another city for the same house.

Some builder-dealers may raise their factory house prices as high as the market will bear. Unfortunately, this can wipe out a good chunk of the savings otherwise possible on a factory house. The builder could sell for less, perhaps. But why do it, the builder asks, when local stickbuilt houses sell for more? In the future, however, as more and more factory houses hit the market, the increased competition may force lower markups. Your best defense now, like getting a good price on other merchandise, is to shop around for the greatest savings.

Finally, savings on factory houses can vary according to local construction costs and prices for stickbuilt houses. The higher the cost to build a stickbuilt house, naturally the higher its sales price will be. And local construction costs fluctuate considerably from one place to another. Factory house prices are more uniform nationally. Thus, you can save more on a factory house in an area of high-cost stickbuilt houses.

One Midwestern home manufacturer president says that getting a good house at an affordable price is one thing in large cities and their suburbs, but often quite another in small towns and rural areas where ". . . there are simply not enough skilled home builders to produce the kind of house people want." Factory houses, particularly those that are made and shipped virtually complete, offer especially welcome savings in such areas.

Factory house savings, on the other hand, may be less in cities and dense suburbs where new houses are built and sold by high-volume builders. In effect, they produce their own efficiently made factory houses, thus at reduced sales prices. The only difference, as noted earlier, is that such a builder's plant or "factory" mass produces only the builder's houses.

■ VACATION HOUSE SAVINGS ■

A manufactured house is clearly a natural for a vacation home. It's a winner in this area. In one swoop, it does away with most of the complications of building a house in a distant rural area, e.g., finding a good builder and skilled workers, to start—not in abundant quantity almost everywhere—and then riding herd on your construction gang by long distance. Most expensive of all, you can easily be a victim of the soak-the-city-slicker syndrome on everything that goes into a vacation house being built stick by stick.

A factory vacation house can clearly save a small bundle of money compared with a stickbuilt house. Because some factory houses especially lend themselves to do-it-yourself completion, greater than usual buyer-builder savings can be made on this score. A factory vacation house often can be completed while you're using it. A number of home manufacturers started in business by turning out vacation houses, and vacation houses from factories are now available nearly everywhere in the country.

■   BUILDING YOUR OWN HOME   ■

You can also save, of course, by building your own home from a factory package or kit. Labor accounts for 16 percent of total house costs (see Chapter 14 for more detail), and building your own factory-made house will help you save on the high cost of labor. Building a house is no easy chore. Don't kid yourself. It takes hard work, though less hard than building a stickbuilt house.

There are other advantages in favor of building a house from a factory package. A factory house can be erected and closed up faster than a stickbuilt house. Hence the likelihood of pilferage and weather damage to the interior is sharply reduced. Factory houses are completed by do-it-yourself labor in six months to a year, or roughly half the usual 1–2½ years that do-it-yourselfers require to complete stickbuilt houses. The time saved can mean money saved, on top of the savings that result by leaving your old house sooner.

Some home manufacturers offer no-down-payment financing that pays for the house parts. They provide, in other words, construction financing, which can be a huge help. Other makers help you obtain a construction loan from a local lender. That's needed because regular mortgage loans are prohibited by law for anything but financing a completed structure. After a house is completed, the construction loan is paid off by means of a mortgage loan, which is then obtainable.

■   THE BIGGEST SAVINGS   ■

You save the most when you buy a mobile home, the lowest-cost house of all. Remember that there are mobile homes and mobile homes. Some of the new ones can take your breath a-way. They are no more like the old house trailer—the Model T of manufactured houses—than an upper-crust residential road resembles shantytown.

However, not all mobile homes are beauties. Many are still boxy, tinny and grim looking. They may be dolled-up with flashy flower pots, wrought iron or other warts that are ill advised. But just as clothing can run across a spectrum from the cheap and gaudy to the attractive, so can mobile homes.

Fortunately, the really good mobile homes do not cost much more than those of questionable design. This applies chiefly to the homes, and not necessarily to mobile home parks and developments. Renting a site in a good mobile home park usually costs more than renting one in a run-of-the-mill park. In some areas of the United States, you also have to shop a little harder and longer to find a good, if not top-quality, mobile home. But it can be worth it.

On average, a mobile home can save as much as 50 percent of the price of a locally built conventional house. In other words, savings run almost half the price of a conventional house. That's based on figures from the U.S. Department of Commerce construction-cost division in Maryland, the acknowledged national oracle for building statistics. In recent years its surveys found that the average cost of a mobile home was approximately $28 per square foot of living area. Average cost of new stickbuilt houses was roughly $50 per square foot, or twice as much. Stickbuilt house costs ranged from some $46 or so per square foot in low-cost areas, up to more than $50 in high-cost areas of the country.

A good mobile home is just about the biggest house bargain anywhere. Where else in the world can you buy a furnished three-bedroom house with central air-conditioning for as little as $25,000?

Answer: Nowhere else.

Incidentally, nearly all mobile homes are mobile only for their brief initial birth period. That's the time from factory completion to overland delivery to the first buyer. Once bought, lowered onto buyers' sites, the wheels taken off and the unit tied down, many mobile homes are never again moved. In addition, a growing number of mobile homes are being anchored down to permanent foundations, like conventional houses. It would take an earthquake to move them again.

How much you can save with a manufactured house depends on the kind of house you buy and the other variables, such as how much do-it-yourself work you do, including running interference for the manufacturer and the local contractors who erect your house. Ask them ahead of time what you can do and how much they will reduce their price for work items you provide; and ask them to put it in writing *before* you buy. In addition to the actual dollars saved, other special advantages of a factory house can add up to money in the bank, major savings that are spelled out in the next chapter.

C·H·A·P·T·E·R   3

Ten Money-Saving Benefits of Manufactured Houses

The factory-made house is a technological accomplishment that was long overdue. The handmade stickbuilt house, by contrast, is as much an anomaly from the dark ages as light from a candle.

Still, the art of efficient mass production of houses in factories is still being perfected. It's in a relatively early stage of its development. Improvements are coming, so don't expect a perfect product now or a rock-bottom price, or both. At this stage of its development, though, the factory house is a big step forward for homebuyers with the following major benefits.

High-quality construction. This ranks well up there in importance with money savings. Top-grade lumber is used in nearly all factory-made houses, largely because second-grade lumber can cause problems with the precision techniques in the plant and thereby slow down production. Most factory houses also are built to conform with the toughest building codes. See Figure 3.1.

Special rigidity and toughness also must be built into factory houses because of the nature of factory-house production, and particularly to withstand the bouncing around encountered during over-the-road shipment. Practically no stickbuilt house

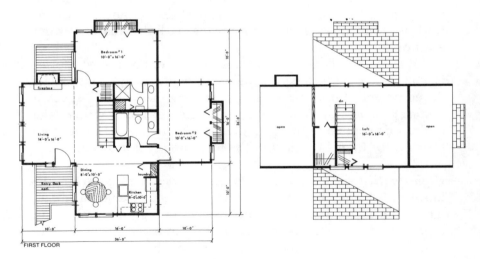

FIRST FLOOR

Figure 3.1 *The vacation house with floor plan (opposite page) and the two-story colonial house above illustrate the wide variety of size and type of houses made by home manufacturers. The attractive vacation house, called the Pedestal 1622, is built to provide both protection from high water in flood plain areas and an expansive waterfront view. The small foundation makes it adaptable to mountain lots, which can also provide spectactualr views. The colonial model is also available with the same floor plan in either contemporary or traditional style. The Colonial:* © *Nationwide Homes, Inc., 1994. All rights reserved. The vacation house and floor plan:* © *Logangate Homes, Inc.*

could stay together, for example, after being lifted into the air and dropped a few times, but many factory houses can. Such strength is overkill, you might say, since Paul Bunyan is not likely to pick up a house, like a ball, and bounce it around. Right?

Wrong. Such punishment could be dished out by a twister, a landslide or an earthquake, and many a factory house can take such a punch like a champion boxer. For example, not long ago a modular house was delivered to its site too late in the day to be anchored down. A tornado lifted the house in the air, spinning it around three times before dropping it to the ground. Peering from their storm cellar, the people next door saw it happen. The next day the assembly crew found the house intact except for dents and broken windows. The house was hauled back in place—it had landed halfway off the foundation—and was anchored down. The dents were repaired, glass was replaced and the house was as good as new. It has been occupied ever since. The maker of the house says that's his answer to the Wizard of Oz.

Another high-quality feature with welcome results is the *kiln-dried* lumber (predried) used in factory houses. One couple did not know about this until a year after moving into their new factory house. A relative in the construction business said, "It's amazing. You have no cracks in your walls. When my new house was a year old, there were cracks all over because of the wood drying out."

That doesn't happen to a factory house because the predried wood does not shrink and warp as a result of uneven drying. Predried wood also means no squeaky floors and no bulging walls and popping nails.

High-quality design. Don't underestimate this one either. A sad fact of life in homebuilding is that professional architects are hired to design only a small minority—perhaps 15 percent—of all conventionally built houses in the United States, according to the American Institute of Architects (AIA). Alas, the haphazard results show it. Many manufactured houses, on the other hand, are designed by architects, including top-notch residential architects. The manufactured house comes with better breeding, which shows in both form and function. That can mean better long-term value, in other words, higher resale value, as well as the day-to-day benefits of living in a better house.

A factory house is no pig in a poke. You know what you're getting and thus no painful surprises later. The same house has been built before and the bugs ironed out. You can often see exactly what you will get by visiting the same house on model-house row outside the factory, or by visiting a previous buyer who owns one. A number of manufacturers will gladly give you the names and addresses of people who have bought homes from them. Beware of the manufacturers who will not. Call, or better yet, visit a few. This can pay off well, since you can find out firsthand how the house has worked out. What should *you* know before you buy? Are there any shortcomings? Any problems to avoid? A past buyer can answer such questions.

Known sales price. The price of a factory house is, unlike putty, usually firm. Few gremlins are likely to torpedo your building costs. Like other consumer products with fixed price tags, it's usually easy to put a firm price on a factory house and stick to it. As many homebuyers ruefully say, building or buying a new stickbuilt house often involves paying extra for cost overruns. (These are not always the builder's fault. They're often due to the crazy-quilt nature of stickbuilt construction.)

Building time is sharply reduced. A factory house often can be delivered and ready to occupy within a month or two months after it's ordered. Sometimes it can be as little as a week or three after the foundation has been completed and the house delivered. That's significant compared with the usual four- to six-month completion time for a stickbuilt house. Getting a stickbuilt house finished even in six months can sometimes be cause for rejoicing, as many a wait-weary buyer can attest.

The time saved on a factory house can mean lower interest costs for the construction loan required to build a house. That's the money that a builder or buyer must usually borrow to finance the building of a house, and a higher interest rate is charged for it than for mortgage loans (which buyers use to finance the purchase of the completed house). This can add up to four-figure savings. Building overhead costs are clearly lower when a house is finished faster.

True, these and other construction savings may be builder costs that end up in the builder's pocket. But just as practically every building cost for a new house is paid for in one way or another by the buyer, savings made are also reflected in the bottom line, i.e., they too usually come back to the buyer. And more directly, the buyer saves by moving into the new house faster, thus leaving behind his or her existing house sooner.

Made-to-order house packages. Some manufacturers will on order turn out a house package built according to a buyer's plans and specifications. They are called *custom* manufacturers. Each will make custom house packages for individual homebuyers, including enough houses to stock a new development for a builder.

There are also *catalog* manufacturers, who turn out a line of houses shown in their catalogs. You may buy any one, often with optional changes, if desired. Many makers will also modify their standard plans on request, though generally this costs extra. Some manufacturers do both. They make their own line of houses shown in their catalogs and on request produce custom house packages for buyers.

Easy financing. Many banks and other mortgage lenders readily approve a mortgage loan on a factory house because the house has been evaluated and financed before. The factory house generally comes with better credentials, including certificates of

Figure 3.2 *Saltbox with deck fits naturally into New England vacation setting. Acorn Structures, Inc. Reprinted with permission.*

approval by state, regional and national building codes. The house construction is clearly acceptable. A buyer might also be blessed with favorable terms, and the mortgage application ordinarily sails through processing. Like any mortgage, the pain comes later when you must pay it back every month.

Building your own factory house from a kit is practically child's play. Okay, it's still hard work. But it's considerably easier than building a stickbuilt house. And, as we noted in Chapter 2, homebuyers can practically call their own signals and pay the manufacturer only for a half-completed shell house, and complete that or any other part of the construction with their own money-saving labor.

Reduced theft and vandalism during construction. As we mentioned in Chapter 2, many factory houses can be closed in and roofed over very quickly, some within a day or two, and therefore locked up quickly. Thus, it's no sitting duck for thieves and vandals, who unfortunately are now major homebuilder vultures. It's a one-day closing-up job for a number of manufacturers. One company official has said, "The same-size stickbuilt house requires up to ten days for the same degree of completion." Closing up a new house fast not only cuts down on theft, but work can start inside at once no matter what the weather.

Sharply reduced waste. Building one house at a time, as many builders do, ". . . can lead to very expensive waste and scrap," said T. W. Cahow, a past president of the National Association of Home Manufacturers (NAHM). He said that leftover wood, nails and broken cartons of materials like flooring and roofing, "are often carted off as scrap, adding nothing to house value, but certainly adding to the cost."

In addition, lumber and other building materials stored outdoors can deteriorate, if not spoil like food, through exposure to the weather. Waste can be kept to a minimum with a factory house because each step of the construction has been planned in advance. The lumber and other materials are supplied in the measured quantities needed.

Figure 3.3 *This red brick house, the Jefferson, is, of all things, a modular house manufactured in Virginia, a slimmed-down modern example of Jeffersonian architecture.* © *Nationwide Homes, Inc. All rights reserved.*

Most factory houses conform with Federal Housing Administration (FHA) standards for houses. That's in addition to conforming with state and regional building codes. It's another step forward because it makes houses eligible for government-insured mortgages, such as the FHA, Department of Veterans Affairs (VA) programs and Farmers Home Loans. It's also a significant plus because meeting FHA standards can also mean easy approval of a private mortgage loan from a private bank or other lender. Many private lenders use FHA construction standards as a basis for approval of the mortgage.

Those are 11 benefits of factory houses—one more than promised. But be realistic. There can also be bad apples among home manufacturers and lemons among the tens of thousands of new factory houses turned out every month; it's inevitable. But the number of bad eggs is far fewer than those encountered among stickbuilt houses because the nature of factory production sharply reduces the chances for mistakes. Wise shopping and careful looking before buying will help you avoid these problems.

Figure 3.4 *Reprinted by permission of Yankee Barn Homes, Inc.*

■ DRAWBACKS AND LIMITATIONS ■

Deep as one may probe, it's hard to find drawbacks with manufactured houses from good manufacturers. In fact, most are actually very well made. Not all, however, may be blue ribbon winners in the good looks department. The worst of all, unfortunately, are some mobile homes that have not progressed much since the Model T days of the breed. Taste, of course, is a personal thing. And there is a wide choice across the spectrum in factory house styles.

The floor plans and room layouts of some manufacturers may offer less variety than stickbuilt houses. This is an occupational hazard in the business because the nature of mass production favors standardization. Nonetheless, manufacturers are beginning to break through such limitations and develop more varied floor plans.

Factory houses are still not sold everywhere, which frustrates many potential buyers. Factory houses are still barred in certain

Figure 3.5 *Energy conservation principles apply to nearly all houses. Plenty of insulation, for example, pays off in houses in every climate. Moreover, good design and orientation to the sun can pay off significantly in houses like the contemporary one above. Reprinted by permission of Northern Counties, Inc.*

cities and towns by arbitrary building codes and other restrictive rules, many of which were written by entrenched local unions, contractors and building-supply power interests. They can't compete with factory houses, so they wage war against them. One place notorious for barring factory houses is New York City, which is cursed by a building code that is a relic of the dark ages. That's one reason why local taxpayers pay dearly for their housing.

How To Tell the Players Without a Scorecard: First, the Modular House

Here and in the next three chapters are profiles of the four main kinds of factory-made houses: modular, panelized, precut and mobile homes. The first three vary chiefly according to the extent each is made in the factory before delivery, and conversely, how much completion work is required after delivery. But once completed after delivery, they all look as if they're from the same mold. Only an expert can tell their different genealogy.

Knowing the basic differences among these four kinds of houses, among other benefits, can help you save the most money on a new house and get the most suitable house for your needs.

■ THE MODULAR HOUSE, ■
CROWN PRINCE OF THE BREED

Also called a sectional house, the modular house could well become the king of housing. It's strong and well built, and made virtually completely in the factory. It's made fast and efficiently and, as a result, usually offers good savings to buyers. Like all factory houses, it's set over a standard foundation, with or without a basement. The modular house is financed by the standard amortized home mortgage in the same way that conventional houses have long been financed.

Like most manufactured houses, most modulars conform with state and regional building codes. Actually, they are built stronger and tougher than virtually any other kind of house, as demonstrated by the minimal damage done to a modular house by the tornado mentioned earlier. Superstrength is built into modulars so that they can endure pounding during long-distance shipping and so they can be lifted bodily by cranes. One expert says that if you, or any unfriendly cyclone, tried to lift the average stickbuilt house, the result would be "instant kindling wood."

■ QUALITY CONTROL ■

A modular house is subject to quality control checks by inspectors at stations along the assembly line. Such control over mishaps is virtually unknown with stickbuilt houses. At the end of the line, a chief inspector, clipboard and checklist in hand, walks through and inspects each item on the list before tagging the house with a completion slip.

Modular and other factory-made houses, by the way, are also inspected during construction in their factories by independent building inspectors, called *third-party inspectors.* On behalf of homebuyers these inspectors ensure that factory-made houses conform to state building codes where they are sold.

The modular house comes off the factory assembly line made in two or more finished sections, usually 12 or 14 feet wide and up to 60 feet or so long. In other words, it's a three-dimensional package. As they come off the assembly line, the sections are loaded on flatbed trucks and head down the highway. Two or more sections are connected together at the site to form a full-fledged house. Additional sections are added to form larger houses, including stacking the sections to make two- or three-story houses, or higher. Once delivered, a modular house can be ready to occupy in a matter of days. That's lightning speed, of course, compared with the months required to finish a stickbuilt house. Outside utility lines for water, gas, electricity and sewage disposal must be connected to the house, of course. The main intake lines for the wiring, plumbing and other utilities inside the house, which were installed in the factory, are capped and are ready for outside hookups.

The delivery time and occupancy date of a modular house obviously depends on preparing the foundation for the house in advance. The foundations for modular houses, like those for other factory houses, must be accurately aligned and level. This is essential or the house will not fit on it properly. If the foundation doesn't conform, you're in trouble.

The word *modular* has to do with a standard basic dimension for the construction of houses. It goes back to Eli Whitney's principle of the interchangeability of parts, which revolutionized factory mass production in the nineteenth century. All the key structural parts of a house conform to a common dimension, such as a 4-inch module or a multiple of it. The different pieces then fit together in different ways, just as the pieces of a child's Tinker Toy set, a marvel of modular design, can fit together and form an enormous variety of little structures.

For a house, a small number of standard modular parts for the floor, walls and roof can fit together in different ways. Using the same modular house parts, therefore, a manufacturer can easily turn out different houses in a variety of sizes and shapes from a small number of the same internal bones and framing pieces. To a homebuyer, that also means that a manufacturer often can modify one of the standard house models at minimal extra cost.

Like most manufactured houses, modulars can be bought in most parts of the United States. Don Carlson, editor and publisher of *Automation in Housing,* has pointed out that all conform to regional and state building codes. As noted above, independent inspectors check them in the factory while they're being built. Conformance with the state building code means that a house usually can be put anywhere in the state, since state codes override local codes, although there are exceptions in cities like New York City, Chicago and Milwaukee.

The development of state-wide building codes is relatively new, but it is already reducing corruption in the building business. Corrupt building inspectors, long a plague, can no longer shake down a home manufacturer by claiming that a house does not conform to the local building code. Often a phony charge, this has long been used to extort money from builders: no payment, no acceptance of the house.

Home manufacturers can now fight back. A New England manufacturer, for example, told me of this problem with houses he shipped to a Boston suburb. A building inspector, seeking a payoff, wouldn't okay the houses even though they conformed with the Massachusetts state building code. The manufacturer appealed to the state code officials. The local inspector was firmly told to shape up. The houses met the code and he could not disallow them.

■ SIZES AND PRICES ■

Modular houses range from modest one-story models with 1,000 square feet of floor area, more or less, up to large models three to four times that size, which is a lot of house. That means finished houses valued from as low as $40,000 to as high as $150,000 or more. Actually, there's no limit to the size and price of modulars. Theoretically, sections can be stacked vertically as well as connected horizontally, which makes available a large variety of house sizes and shapes practically at the push of a button.

As a matter of fact, some manufacturers sell modular housing of two- to four-level buildings with 8–16 individual apartments. As a result, a growing number of multistory apartment houses and condominiums are also being built from factory-made modular sections. Again, most people don't even realize when they're looking at manufactured housing. One of the most famous examples of modular housing and the vistas it opened up is the much-publicized Habitat in Montreal, Canada, designed

Figure 4.1 *Famed Habitat housing complex in Montreal, designed by Israeli architect Moshe Safdie, is the classic demonstration of modular housing. Individual sections were built in a nearby plant, trucked to the site, and lofted into place by a crane. Moshe Safdie & Associates.*

by Israeli architect Moshe Safdie, and unveiled at the 1968 Montreal Exposition.

■ DESIGN AND FLOOR PLANS ■

This brings up an early criticism of the modular house: not enough design variety. Part of the trouble arises because individual house sections are made no wider than 12 or 14 feet. Depending on the state, that's the maximum width or "wide load" permitted for house delivery trucks on the highways. At last count, all states allowed 14-foot wides. Even if shipped by rail, trucks are required for final delivery, so no factory house sections wider than 12 or 14 feet are usually made. One notable exception occurs in various western states where full-width houses are commonly shipped short distances from the factory to the chosen site.

Room sizes are often no wider than these dimensions, though the houses may be two to three times the width of each section. That's accomplished by assembling two or three rectangular sections side by side. The total size and number of rooms is determined by the length of each section, which can range up to about 60 feet. Two 14-foot sections, side by side, each 70 feet long, can produce a good-sized house of 1,960 square feet. A house that is twice this size, or nearly 4,000 square feet of living space, can be made by stacking two more sections on top for a two-story house. Because some highway rules mandate that factory house sections be no more than 12 or 14 feet wide, it does not, however, downgrade the architectural design and livability of a modular house. As noted later, even a maximum room width of only 12 feet adequately meets the minimum architectural standards for good design for every room of a house.

There's also good news on the modular floor-plan front. Modular house designers have begun to break through old design barriers. Floor plans are being varied by adding a third or fourth section at a right angle to the main house to produce an L- or T-shaped plan. More and more houses wider than 28 feet are being made with three sections. These are designed to give triple-wide houses. In short, the modular house may originally have had plan limitations, but new ones offer greater variety.

■ MAXIMUM SAVINGS WITH A MODULAR HOUSE ■

Savings depend on the brand and those other variables, cited earlier, that affect prices. The largest savings possible with modular houses are less than the savings possible with mobile homes mainly because modular houses are built to conform to tougher, more demanding building codes and modulars require more expensive foundations.

The primary fact is that the modular house is probably the best, strongest and most efficiently made house in the world today. Anyone who doubts this should be reminded of foreigners who are ordering U.S. modulars despite hefty cost increases for overseas shipment. The cost of modular houses also could come down in the future as more and more of them are made and sold. As new methods of making and selling them are developed and manufacturers swing into high gear, greater savings could inevitably follow, especially as more and more people wake up to the reasons for their growing popularity. Saving the most money on a modular house still requires the same effort required for top savings when buying anything else, from steak to cars: Comparison shop.

■ A FEW FINAL QUESTIONS OFTEN ASKED ■

Exactly how do you finance a modular house? Much the same way that any regular house is financed. Often the manufacturer or a local representative can recommend a mortgage lender who knows the house and will give you a mortgage. But you should still shop among other mortgage lenders, too. Compare the different terms offered. By the way, many homebuyers overlook a major way to save on this score. They don't know that shopping for a good mortgage can be important, since mortgages can vary in cost and content.

What about resale value? Like any other good house, modular house values should increase in the future as they have in the past, assuming that overall housing values continue to rise. But just as the best cars attract the highest resale value, the resale value of modular houses should rise higher than that of typical stickbuilt houses. That's because of the higher quality of modulars.

C·H·A·P·T·E·R 5

The Panelized House

With the exception of mobile homes, more panelized houses are turned out by manufacturers every month than any other kind of factory house. More homebuyers therefore are likely to buy a panelized house than any other kind of factory house. It's a house made by scores of different manufacturers. It comes in a wide variety of types, sizes, plans and styles—from low-priced beer models, up to high-priced champagne models, and plenty of variety in between.

Panelized means that the complete walls of a house are factory-made in large sections, or panels, usually 8 feet high and up to 40 feet long. Sometimes the doors and windows are factory-installed in the wall panels, which is called *prehung*. The panels are designed to go up quickly, immediately after delivery, one after the other. Then the structure can be quickly topped with the roof, closed and locked up within a few days—sometimes by nightfall of the first day. Work still has to be finished inside, to be sure, but getting a house locked up that fast is one of the major accomplishments of factory-made houses.

Some manufacturers also provide a panelized floor system or a roof system made in panels for fast installation, or both, supplied with their packages.

■ ADVANTAGES ■

A panelized house may not save you as much time and money as a modular house. But for that trade-off, it offers these advantages:

1. You can choose from a great variety of floor plans.
2. Most can be modified to suit a buyer's needs.
3. Savings to buyers, including professional builders and developers, who want factory houses made from their own plans and specifications. Many manufacturers will turn out one or many panelized houses for any buyer.
4. Do-it-yourself buyers can save time and money by doing their own building from a sophisticated house kit instead of going through the agony of building a whole house from scratch.
5. Savings are possible on a vacation house that fits any of the first four categories above.

■ HOW GOOD A HOUSE IS IT? ■

Like most manufactured houses, panelized houses conform with state and regional building codes. As a result, they are usually better-made than required by most local building codes. There may be a few exceptions, since not every apple in a barrel is perfect. Number One lumber and high-grade materials are used. Workmanship is usually excellent since it's a consequence of factory fabrication. Parts are put together in forms and jigs, which lock them into place like the mold for baking a cake. Also, there's little room for sloppiness because of the quality control over the assembly-line production of panelized houses.

Good workmanship does not always extend to the completion of houses at the site because site construction is more susceptible to human errors. To avoid site mistakes, some manufacturers send their own factory crews to assemble their houses.

The greater the number of house parts made in a factory, the less labor is required at the site. Thus, less likelihood of sloppy work and mistakes creeping in when the house is being finished.

Figure 5.1 *Here are the main stages of the construction of a panelized factory house. The foundation obviously must be made prior to delivery. After delivery, the prefabbed wall panels are bolted and nailed in place, and the roof house is closed up with roof panels. The complete shell can be finished in a matter of days, depending on the house, and the house completed in a matter of weeks. Acorn Structures, Inc. Reprinted with permission.*

The on-site construction location of a new house is like a battleground, a vulnerable place. The less action there, the better.

■ **THE PANELIZED PACKAGE** ■

The package is known in the trade as "the wood." Its contents from the factory vary from manufacturer to manufacturer. In addition to panelized walls, it usually contains the prefabricated parts for the basic structure of the house, i.e., floor, ceiling and roof. The outside doors and windows are supplied separately, if not installed in the wall panels. Some manufacturers provide little more to complete the house. The house buyer provides the rest. Other makers provide more, including kitchens and bathrooms, heating, wiring and plumbing.

One small manufacturer, for example, supplies panelized wall sections for its houses, but only precut parts for the floor, ceiling and roof. The 4" × 10" floor girder, floor joists and subfloor plywood panels are provided cut to size, but they must

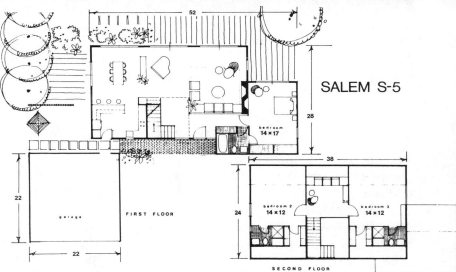

Figure 5.2 *This 2,100 square foot house is sited for convenient entry, but privacy for the residents inside. Large glass areas in the rear open up to a delightful outdoor vista. Reprinted by permission of Habitat/American Barn Corp.*

be nailed together at the site. Windows and doors are supplied with the wall panel system, but the interior partitions are made from bundles of precut framing supplied with the package. Other parts supplied with the package include roof trusses, sheathing and shingles; roof flashing and gutters; stairs, including railings; hardware, which means nails, screws, plates, and bolts; kitchen and bathroom cabinets; and interior trim and doors. Cedar interior paneling and fireplace are optional. All else must be provided by the buyer.

The package made and sold by a large midwestern manufacturer illustrates a more complete factory house package. It is designed to cut building costs by sharply speeding up on-site erection. It provides the complete floor, wall, ceiling and roof panel systems. The wiring and insulation are factory-installed inside the wall panels. Kitchen-bathroom cores are made as a unit and shipped with each package. Much of the rest of the house is also supplied. Chapter 6 lists what you get in a well-furnished house package together with specifications. Just about the only significant difference between that package and what is supplied with a panelized house is that for the panelized house the walls, and sometimes the floor and roof systems, are made and supplied in large panels.

■ "OPEN" VERSUS "CLOSED" PANELS ■

These terms refer to the degree of completion of the wall panels for a panelized house. These panels are either open or closed. A house delivered with closed panels is more complete when it leaves the factory. Its panels are shipped containing insulation, wiring and electrical outlets, all installed in the factory and closed on both sides. The exterior wall siding (outer skin) closes the outside, and the finished interior wall surface (a skin of gypsum board or paneling) closes the inside. Once closed-panel walls are erected, usually in a day or so, the outer shell of the house is not only closed up but complete.

A house with open panels obviously requires more time and on-site work to finish. Open-panel walls are made with only their outside surface cover installed in the factory; the inside is open and hollow. Insulation, wiring, interior skin and anything else needed are put in the walls after the panels are in place. Only then can the inside of the walls be closed; that's usually with gypsum board.

A house with closed panels can save time and money, with one exception. Closed walls are made in the factory considerably faster and better. Fewer things are likely to go wrong in the factory, compared with the site where gremlins abound. The house with closed walls is, in short, more efficiently made. Besides, the manufacturers who turn out closed-panel houses clearly strive for a more advanced and sophisticated product. This is reflected in their houses being more advanced and sophisticated.

The exception is an open-panel house for do-it-yourself buyers who want to save money by using their own labor to complete the house. The extra time required to complete the house is less important. They thrive on squeezing globs of insulation inside the walls, threading the wiring through and closing up the panels. The more, the merrier, since all the additional labor provided by the buyer is money in his or her bank.

■   THE PANELIZED HOUSE SUMMED UP   ■

Compared with modular and mobile homes, a panelized house may save you less money, but it offers greater design variety. Because the panelized house is less completely made in the factory, it requires more on-site construction. Finding skilled people to complete its construction may pose a problem. This is easily overcome in an area where the manufacturer can supply a skilled factory crew to complete on-site construction of the houses. However, it can be more difficult in other places. Completion of a panelized house in particular requires erection crews with precision know-how and experience.

Compared with a precut house, on the other hand, a panelized house ordinarily can save you more money because it requires less on-site construction labor. This, though, can make a panelized house less attractive to do-it-yourself buyers who welcome a house kit that requires plenty of on-site labor. These buyers fairly drool for every chance to use their own labor to save money. A panelized house can still be their cup of tea. But all except the most skilled homebuyers should probably step aside to let professionals erect the structural shell of a panelized house. And then, perhaps, they can step in to complete the rest of the house by themselves. Many panelized houses are, in fact, built and sold by manufacturers' builder-dealers, some on order from buyers, others built speculatively.

C·H·A·P·T·E·R 6

The Precut House

The precut house comes in a broad variety of sizes and types, and the quality of its materials can be quite high. But it is the factory house least completed in the factory. It is, in effect, the least educated factory house, a grade-school graduate at most. Because it requires the most on-site construction labor to finish after delivery, the quality of the finished house can't be guaranteed. It depends on how well its builder does the job at the site. Figure 6.1 shows one type of precut house.

Also, because of the relatively large amount of on-site construction work it requires, it offers the least potential for buyer savings, with the major exception of the do-it-yourself buyer for whom the precut house kit glows with money-saving appeal. It is the largest put-it-together-yourself kit of any kind available.

Offering maximum savings to do-it-yourself homebuyers is one of its main advantages. Just about the only other time a precut house makes sense is to obtain a special kind of factory house (log or dome home, for example) that is available only in a precut package. Usually the only alternative way to get a special house like one of those is to build it from scratch.

Figure 6.1 *Multi-level house with three bedrooms and 2,300 square feet of living area is ideally designed for hilly land. Acorn Structures, Inc. Reprinted with permission.*

The main drawbacks and limitations of precut houses? Two have been noted: the comparatively small potential for saving time and money they offer (again except for the do-it-yourself buyer), and the greater susceptibility to on-the-job errors because so much of it is built at the site. A number of precut manufacturers do, however, provide traveling factory work crews to assemble their houses. Naturally, you pay their travel time.

■ THE PACKAGE INGREDIENTS ■

A precut house package, "the wood" generally contains all or most of the lumber for the main structure of a house, from floor to roof. The outside doors and windows are generally included. But after that, there is no set type or quantity of package ingredients. It varies from barebones kits of precut wood on the one extreme, to bigger kits containing practically everything needed to build a house, including the kitchen sink.

Here are two examples: First is the barebones package sold by a New England maker, Timberpeg. It contains the precut lumber for the structural shell of the company's natural wood houses, which means floor, wall and roof system, including shingles, insulation, windows and exterior doors. Nearly all of the rest of the house must be provided by the buyer, including foundation, basement stairs, interior partitions, all kitchen and bathroom parts and, among other things, the plumbing, heating, wiring and lighting. Why buy such a package when the buyer must provide so much of the house? Because houses like this one can offer something special in their distinctive design, and the prefabricated structural parts supplied by the manufacturer do represent a major lift over building a new house from scratch.

The second example is a package with virtually all the ingredients needed for a house. For example, a package can include the following:

- Floor system with steel bridging

- Wall system with prehung doors and windows (which means the windows and doors are preset in their frames at the factory)

- Exterior siding (outside skin)

- Gypsum board for the inside wall skin

- Roof-ceiling system including roof shingles, gutters, downspouts, flashing for the chimney and plumbing vents

- Interior partitions, doors and closet shelving

- Kitchen cabinets, countertop, fixtures, appliances, exhaust hood and fan and vinyl flooring

- Bath(s) medicine cabinet, sink, tub, toilet, shower stall and ceramic tile

- Household hardware (door knobs, locks and hinges)

- Electric heating system, with a thermostat for each room

- Hot water heater, 200-ampere capacity, central electric board and wiring package for all circuits

- "Rough" plumbing consisting of water lines for the kitchen and bathroom fixtures (but not the main plumbing supply and drain pipe system, which is one of the few major things besides the foundation not provided by the manufacturer). Figure 6.2 shows a sample listing of everything supplied with this package.

Between these two extreme examples of precut house packages, other manufacturers supply varied assortments of parts for their houses. Obviously, the more complete the package, the easier and faster it is to complete the house. Time and money also can be saved when a house package includes materials like roofing shingles, insulation and items such as nails. A package with such sundries gives you the right amount of measured quantities of each for the house. Buying the same things from a local lumber yard could easily mean overkill, hence overpaying for things left over, also called waste. If in doubt about this, get bids from local lumber yards for the same materials, and compare them with the prices charged by the house manufacturer. Comparing costs may sound like a big pain, but it can reduce your spending.

Figure 6.2 What You Can Get With a Precut Factory House Package

EXTERIOR

Steel Adjustable Columns per Plan

Framing

Floor Joists   2″ × 8″ or 2″ × 10″ on 16″ centers with steel bridging, ready to install for extra rigidity. 2″ × 6″ foundation sill plates and 6″ × 10″ built-up main beam.

Wall Framing   2″ × 4″ on 16″ centers. All corners include 2″ × 4″ built-up corner studs. All window openings supported by two 2″ × 10″ headers.

Wall Sheathing   ½″ thick 4′ × 8′ plywood on all exterior corners, ½″ asphaltic impregnated sheathing for increased structural rigidity.

Ceiling Joists   2″ × 6″ on 16″ centers precut and beveled. 2″ × 4″ stay board supplied for leveling, spacing and stiffening each span of ceiling joists.

Roof Rafters   2″ × 6″ on 16″ centers precut and notched, supported by a 2″ × 8″ ridge board and tied together by 1″ × 6″ collar beams.

Gable Wall   2″ × 4″ on 16″ centers with ½″ asphaltic impregnated sheathing, 2″ × 6″ plate.

Roofing

Sheathing   ½″ thick 4′ × 8′ plywood.

Shingles   Asphalt shingles over 15 lb. asphalt saturated felt. Self-seal for extra weather protection with 15-year guarantee. Aluminum roof edging.

Gutter and Downspout   5″ K-type aluminum (white) gutter with 2″ × 3″ downspout and accessories.

Flashing   Aluminum flashing included for all valleys.

Exterior Wall Finish

Siding   White horizontal double 4″ with aluminum continuous corners or vertical primed manufactured siding.

Trim   Aluminum (white) soffit, fascia and barge system. Aluminum soffit vents, rafter baffles and vinyl gable louvers.

Millwork

Doors   1¾″ thick steel insulated, primed and prehung front and rear doors. Hardware and weather stripping supplied, drip cap where applicable. Aluminum threshold installed.

Windows   Primed white pine double-hung (or slider where specified) factory assembled with balances and weather stripping, ready to be set into the wall. Window and door blinds are included where specified. Caulking.

Storm Windows   Aluminum (white) combination storm/screen windows for double hung windows. Storm panels and screens for sliding windows.

Interior

Walls

Framing   All partitions, bearing and nonbearing are precut 2″ × 4″ on 16″ centers for 8 feet ceiling height with double top plates. Semi-assembled door bucks with two 2″ × 10″ headers.

Insulation   R-11 rating for floors over unheated areas and exterior walls and R-19 for ceiling area. Sill sealer, box joist insulation, insulation at exterior corners and intersecting interior and exterior partitions.

Wall Covering   Polyethylene vapor barrier on exterior walls. Choice of ½″ drywall board in 4′ × 8′ or 4′ × 12′ sheets complete with spackling cement, joint tape, and metal corner beads. In the bathrooms, your choice of colors in ceramic wall tile in the tub or shower alcove, 6 feet high from the floor.

Doors

Passage doors are semi-assembled prehung mahogany flush with hinges installed, center bored for lockset. Each closet has mahogany flush wood sliding doors.

Millwork

Trim   Solid, clear-grade, white pine casings for windows and doors, door stops, baseboard and floor molding. Pin rails, shelving and rod supports for all closets included.

Stairways   Basement stairway includes handrail, post, precut stringers, risers and treads. Where specified, finished stairway is preassembled, prefit, and predrilled (oak optional). It includes fir or yellow pine treads and risers, newel, handrail, balusters and other accessories applicable.

Flooring

Subfloor   ½" thick 4' × 8' plywood sheathing for strong floor platform.

Finished Floor   Choice of two styles of carpeting over ⅜" urethane padding over ⅝" particle board underlayment or 25/32" × 2¼" #1 oak hardwood flooring, tongue and grooved and end matched over red rosin building paper. In kitchen and bath areas, choice of vinyl asbestos floor tile over ⅝" plywood underlayment or vinyl cushioned flooring over ⅝" particleboard underlayment.

Hardware

Nails   An adequate supply of nails of all sizes and types required in accordance with standard building procedures.

Finished Hardware   Brass finish door locks, hinges, door stops, sash locks, handrail brackets and aluminum closet rods.

Plumbing

Rough   "PVC" or "ABS" plastic drainage system complete with fittings and ½" M copper tubing water lines with all fittings.

Finish   Fixtures include a 24" vanity with one-piece molded top, scalloped bowl and molded backsplash, plus water closet— in your choice of colors with a matching seat and cover. Family bathroom includes tub with shower; master bathroom features stall shower with tempered safety glass enclosure, plus water closet and 24" vanity. Powder room includes water closet, wall hung lavatory and rectangular mirror medicine cabinet with bar light. Shutoff valves below all sinks and water closets.

Bathroom Accessories   Deluxe oval mirror/medicine cabinet and deluxe light fixture. Also chrome towel bar, toothbrush and tumbler holder, soap and grab bar, paper holder and shower curtain rod.

Heating

System   Electric baseboard

heating system with individual room thermostats. System designed for local heating requirements.

Hot Water   52-gallon glass-lined, electric, quick-recovery domestic hot water heater with safety relief valve.

Electric

Rough   200-Amp service with switch-type circuit breaker panel. All necessary ceiling and wall boxes per the current National Electrical Code.

Wire   Wire package includes sufficient amount of 12/2 and 14/2 copper wire and breakers to complete all house circuits per plan. Also, proper size and amount of wire and breakers are supplied to install all appliances and utilities.

Finish   Your choice of several styles of lighting fixtures. All necessary receptacles, switches, plates and accessories are included. Bedrooms, dens and family rooms have switched receptacles. Door chimes provided. Smoke detector provided for each sleeping area.

Kitchen

Cabinets   Your choice of cabinets in hand-rubbed oak finish. All wall cabinets feature adjustable shelves.

Sink and Counter Top   Choice of stainless steel or colored single bowl sink with all fittings and faucet. The countertop is post-formed Formica in your choice of pattern and color.

Appliances   30-inch freestanding electric or gas range with removable oven door; dishwasher; M-4 ductless range hood with fan, light, and charcoal filter in a pre-assembled, prewired unit; hood.

Note: Some parts supplied in a house package (kit) like this may be omitted or substitutions made, and sometimes additional parts may be supplied at the customer's option. Understandably, the specific products supplied will change from time to time. Though this shows what's supplied in a bulging precut house package, much the same contents may be supplied with a panelized house except that the walls and sometimes the floor and ceiling systems are made in long panels, usually with prehung windows and doors. Others come with fewer parts for the house, and some with more.

■   THE UTILITIES   ■

Plumbing, heating and wiring kits supplied with some precut packages can simplify these mechanical installations, but move cautiously here. For one thing, be sure that the plumbing and wiring will pass your local building code. Most do meet or exceed accepted national standards. The wiring in manufactured houses, for example, usually will pass the National Electrical Code. But that's not good enough for some building inspectors. A similar code conflict could cause a problem with the plumbing in a house package. Avoid this by checking on it beforehand. By comparison, the house structure itself usually meets or exceeds state and building codes and poses less of a problem.

For another thing, the decision whether to accept the optional plumbing, heating and electrical wiring with a precut package can be influenced by the people who will install each in the house. If you must depend on local contractors for this, see them beforehand. Will they install the equipment supplied by the manufacturer? Contractors often buck at this because not supplying the equipment costs them the opportunity to make more money, on both the materials and the installation. And it's partly because some contractors don't want to install equipment with which they're not familiar. They don't know how. If you're going to install such things yourself, taking what the manufacturer offers with the package can simplify things for you. If not, you can avoid problems with your contractor by being sure about the installation before ordering the house package.

■ OPTIONAL CHANGES ■

The options offered with precut packages break down into two categories, much like those offered with panelized houses: design (change-of-plan) and material options. The first deals with altering the original plan, for example, having a manufacturer add a room or two, say, to one of the standard models you like, or merely putting in a sliding glass door. These changes usually can be made though they may cost extra.

The second, material options, has to do with your choice brand and color of the materials supplied with a house. Examples include a choice of wall materials, such as horizontal or vertical wall siding; different kinds of windows and appliances, and so on. There is usually no extra charge for these except for an option chosen that costs decidedly more than another; if it costs decidedly less, you should get a credit.

Another category of options is less well known. It is obtaining special-quality products, particularly those that will pay high dividends in savings and economy. These are things like extra insulation and double- or triple-pane insulating glass or top-quality brand products like Andersen windows or a Kitchenaid dishwasher, two of the best for their respective uses. Other high-quality products like these are discussed later.

■ SHIPPING DISTANCES ■

Unlike other factory houses, some manufacturers will ship their precut houses long distances. Some makers ship their packages anywhere in the country and overseas, too. This can be done because the precut package contains less of a house than other factory packages; therefore it weighs less and its long-distance shipping costs are not as high. As noted earlier, though, be sure that a house shipped beyond the manufacturer's normal marketing area meets your local building code.

To sum up, the precut house is half a loaf or less because much of the material for it has to be provided by the buyer and more of it has to be built at the site, compared with other factory houses. The precut house can be a boon for do-it-yourself buyers who want to save a lot of money by using their own construction labor. Precut houses include well-designed houses and special houses that are unavailable elsewhere in the factory house field.

C·H·A·P·T·E·R 7

Log, Dome and A-Frame Houses

This is a trio of special houses that can now be had in precut factory-made packages. In other words, these houses are sub-categories of the precut factory house. Anyone who still builds one from scratch, not from a factory package, should have his head examined.

Log cabins, chalets and lodges have always been popular in Canada and have enjoyed a surge in popularity in the United States beginning in the 1970s. Though widely used for vacation houses out in the woods, their natural habitat, more and more are now being built—by do-it-yourselfers as well as contractors—for year-round living. And you don't have to be a pioneer to live in one!

They're made in many styles and factory-made with varied construction techniques. Though well suited for rugged backwoods terrain, they no longer demand rugged living within. These houses not only have electricity and central heat, if desired; some models are equipped with cathedral ceilings, porches, dormers, lofts, skylights and even a matching doghouse.

Log houses seem particularly appealing these days because of our collective nostalgia for the way things were, because they have rustic looks and handcrafted appeal, because they're quick and inexpensive to build and because they come in factory-made kits. Since they require neither framing nor siding, they go up quickly and require little in the way of maintenance—an occasional coating of preservative, indoors and out, as a substitute for paint. See Figure 7.1 for an example of a log house.

Unless you choose one of the few double-walled structures with insulation between the log layers, what you see on the outside is what you get on the inside: solid timber walls as thick as desired, usually from six to eight inches thick. Solid timber construction, moreover, is long lasting. The owner of one log-building school says, "A log house, if built correctly and preserved properly (given periodic coats of preservative), should last

Figure 7.1 *Not every log house looks like the cabin where Abe Lincoln was born. Reprinted by permission of Alta Industries, Ltd., designers and manufacturers of Alta Log Homes.*

for 250 years." A log-building school is just as it says: a school for teaching builders and others how to put together a log house. Many are inexpensive and give fast courses. Names of schools near you can be located from a log house manufacturer.

Though log houses offer most of the conveniences demanded by contemporary homeowners, the energy efficiency of many is "a sticky question," according to Terry Sherwood of the U.S. Forest Products Laboratory, a government research group. Some may even offer fuel savings; occupants of log structures boast of low utility bills. Supposedly, a log house can be adequately heated by a good airtight wood-burning stove, and log house makers claim that it will retain heat better and use less energy than an equivalently sized frame house. Most log houses do meet most regional and local codes. A number of them are also approved for Federal Housing Administration (FHA) and Department of Veterans Affairs (VA) financing. But in some areas, uninsulated log walls may not meet energy-code requirements for insulated walls.

Experts point out that solid wood, as in log walls, is not a top insulator. Nonetheless, a solid log wall six to eight inches thick is equivalent to an ordinary house wood-stud wall with up to two inches of insulation. That's not bad, considering that the first inch or two of insulation saves the most heat.

In addition, the log house people say that national energy standards for houses do not give credit to a log house for its heat absorption and thermal storage capacity. This claim was, on the whole, confirmed by research at the U.S. government's National Bureau of Standards (NBS). It found that the heat absorption of logs and their high storage capacity benefit the occupants of a log house the most in spring and fall. Then a log house can be easier to heat and save energy, compared with a conventional house. In summer, the storage effect works in reverse and keeps you cooler.

In winter, though, the heat storage of logs does not necessarily pay off so well, according to the NBS research. So in a very cold winter climate, adding insulation to log walls may be desirable for comfort and energy efficiency. If in doubt about this, check with a few owners of log houses where you intend to build.

In some houses, heat efficiency is beefed up by slipping insulation in the log walls. Other solutions are offered by manufacturers to produce a high enough R-value to meet stiff code requirements. (The R-value rating measures the resistance of a material to the transmission of heat; the higher the R-value, the greater the insulation.) One maker's logs are hollowed out; the dead air within allegedly insulates better than solid timber, though this is questionable, too. Other logs contain insulating fiberglass or urethane. Some logs are joined with gaskets that form airtight, watertight seals. Some log walls are built with nails or spikes, some with splines. Some use traditional chinking. Some require caulking. Some combine any number of these methods. And some manufacturers' precision-cut logs fit together so tightly with saddle notches construction that the blade of a knife cannot pass between them.

There are other choices to make as well. The timber used can be cedar, pine, fir, poplar, spruce or other types. Northern white cedar is the gem of the bunch and is the best insulator. The U.S. Forest Products Laboratory rates cedar, spruce, pine and fir, in that order, as the most desirable for log houses. Logs are either hand peeled or machine peeled, air dried or kiln dried. They may be left rounded, flattened top and bottom or hollowed to fit onto the adjacent logs. Most, however, have grooves to accommodate electrical wiring. Some are dipped in preservative to repel rot, mold, insects and rodents; cedar by itself has natural resistance to bugs (including termites) and to rot.

With any construction system, precut log homes in kit form can be erected by the buyer or by a local builder. Some manufacturers ship only logs cut to conform to the buyer's blueprints. In general, even the most expensive log cabins will cost less than a standard wood-frame house. Because of the variety of packages available, cost comparisons between log-house kits are hard to give. While the price of a kit-built log shell is invitingly low, construction costs can double or triple the bill.

Factory packages don't include the foundation, and rarely the roof, flooring, heating, plumbing or wiring, so finishing the house adds considerably to the cost. Some kits include doors and windows, while other manufacturers advise buying these locally.

Labor is obviously an important factor in determining the construction cost of a house. Doing the major construction oneself can save between a quarter and a half of the finished value of a house, says one industry expert.

To lower your building cost, look for a good company with a nearby factory. After all, the shorter the distance the logs must travel, the lower the shipping expenses. Determine how much of the building you can do and how much help you'll have. Then figure the contracting cost of having the foundation built, the walls installed and so on. Find out which components are cheaper locally and which should be ordered from the manufacturer.

Warning: Before you start, of course, check that your local building code permits a log house, and arrange for the financing. A house that you can neither pay for nor live in is no bargain. A surprising number of supposedly intelligent people have had to find this out the hard way.

■ THE DOME HOUSE ■

The dome house is Buckminster Fuller's geodesic dome, designed to stretch a minimum of material over the maximum area. It is one of the strongest structures ever built. On a cost-per-foot basis, it could be the cheapest, too. Moreover, a dome is adaptable, easy to build and inexpensive to live in. But though this geometric masterpiece provides unique shelter, it also demands a unique lifestyle, and it could keep the wrong owners running around in circles.

The traditional geodesic dome is composed of flat plane triangles bolted together to form curved pentagons. Because of the inherent strength of the triangle, it is ideal housing in an earthquake or tornado area. The wooden or metal framework is covered with either a canvas or plastic skin or with wooden panels. The structure is self-supporting; no interior walls or posts are required (though load-bearing walls must be added to support a second or third story for sleeping lofts). Figure 7.2 provides an example of a dome house.

Figure 7.2 *As with other manufacturers, the makers of dome houses offer you custom options. Reprinted by permission of Oregon Dome, Inc.*

The house may be erected on what's called a riser wall, or it may rest on a foundation, with or without a basement. As many as ten skylights are incorporated in some models, and five trapezoidal areas around the base can accommodate windows or doors; two or more domes often are attached along these openings.

Sizes vary from small one-floor dome houses of about 26 feet in diameter to large, elaborate houses with two or three levels and a diameter of 45 feet. The 35-foot diameter dome contains 1,740 square feet of living area over two stories. The 39-foot dome, perhaps the most common, offers 2,200 square feet, or a lot of house, over two levels and is 16 feet high at its center (the best location, by the way, for a fireplace).

Depending on size, dome represents about 25 percent of the finished cost of a complete dome. Sold nationally through builder-dealers, domes are 5 to 15 percent cheaper to build than conventional houses. One builder claims that it costs about 10 percent less per square foot to build. Recently, dome costs ran about $40 per square foot. A simple structure was about $30 per square foot, while a more lavish dome could be about $35. A complete geodesic dome house can cost as little as $30,000. But a special exterior adds to the cost, and many buyers demand extras like decks, dormers, and additional skylights to lower lighting costs. Fuel bills, by the way, can run 30 to 50 percent less than those for heating a conventional house of the same size; because a dome has less surface area, less heat is lost.

Of course, a do-it-yourself buyer can cut the cost considerably, as with other house packages. One dome manufacturer estimates that 75 percent of his customers do all the work on the shell, and 25 percent do almost all of the rest, too. Though an unskilled buyer is not advised to undertake the foundation or install the roofing, plumbing, wiring or heating, the shell construction is relatively simple even for amateurs. The mass-produced parts are designed for on-site assembly, and a whole dome can be completed in one to three days after the foundation is ready. Some kits contain preassembled panels to expedite work.

As mentioned earlier, the price of a dome kit, or package, depends on various factors, including distance from the maker's plant, its size and the materials included. In addition to the framework, most packages include the skin and some provide the wall-roof insulation. Some makers offer canopies and other light openings such as transoms and skylights. Occasionally, interior paneling is included and roof sealant almost always should be included.

Sealant raises a problem that can confront domeowners— leakage. Though companies provide waterproofing, it can be less than efficient. Thus it rains indoors when it's raining outside, an unwelcome happening. Tar and webbing over seams can work. For assured nonleakage, a regular roofing cover like asphalt or fiberglass shingles, wood shingles or shakes is recommended. One roofing method is a spray-on insulant covered with a rubberized roofing material. Finishing the interior can be expensive because most commonly used materials are geared for rooms with right angles.

Other drawbacks to dome living can be considered pluses by others who like life in the round. Decorating offers interesting problems; if you want to hang a picture on a wall, you may have to add the wall. There is much flexibility in the division of space, but the fewer partitions added, the less air-space patterns will be blocked. Acoustics within a dome are marvelous, which is wonderful for music appreciation, but perhaps less wonderful for privacy.

As domes grow more popular, the nitty-gritty of codes and financing is easier to deal with, especially since some domes are approved by the FHA and the VA. Still, they can present problems. In fact, a dome might meet even more resistance than a log house because it is less conventional. But building codes should not be troublesome, particularly if the structure is professionally built. Some manufacturers provide engineering drawings to demonstrate the structural soundness of their products. Lending institutions probably won't be difficult to convince, either, but obviously you must check before ordering a dome.

■   THE A-FRAME HOUSE   ■

Initially designed for the cold north, particularly in ski country, A-frame houses were to the 1950s what the dome was to the 1980s, an innovative, inexpensively built form of architecture suitable for those who don't mind—or emphatically desire—an open, airy, contemporary house. Like the geodesic dome, the A-frame yields shaped living quarters without right-angled walls.

Viewed head-on, an A-frame structure looks like what it's called, a letter A; or an inverted V. As in a dome, roof and walls are one and inseparable, and the interior space is open and airy. The steep roof makes the A-frame ideal in heavy snow areas; snow slides off. The angle of the roof also minimizes wind damage, leakage and maintenance work, and it results in a longer house life. See Figure 7.3 for an example.

An A-frame house is inexpensive to build because the strong roof members double as the wall framing. To cut costs further,

Figure 7.3 *The Swiss chalet is the forerunner of this A-frame house. House package by American Timber Homes, Escanaba, MI.*

this style is available in modular form. One manufacturer offers a modest single-wide A-frame, 13' × 36', thus 468 square feet of living space. Two double-wide designs, 22' × 36' and 22' × 40', give you 792 square feet and 880 square feet respectively. The square-foot areas are given only for ground floors. Each can include a second story, and an optional basement can provide even more room. An A-frame house designed for vacations and weekends, as so many are, frequently offers a cathedral ceiling and a sleeping loft that occupies only half the upper space. The A-frame house can be an exciting place that is surprisingly airy and open, and it feels twice as large as it actually is.

The total cost of an A-frame house should run about 10 percent less than a house with conventional walls and roof. The largest savings, of course, are due to consolidating the walls and roof, and the simplified interior. However, plumbing is plumbing, heating is heating and wiring is wiring, so the cost of these is about as much as those for a conventional wall-roof house.

Like a dome house, an A-frame should be insulated to the hilt. Its roof-wall structure needs as much insulation as the roof of a regular house. And its doors and windows should be equally well insulated.

C·H·A·P·T·E·R 8

Mobile Homes

Forget everything you've heard about mobile homes—start fresh and take them on their own terms. They have many faces, and some are surprisingly attractive.

True, many poor cousins among them are far from good looking, and some of the places where they stand are little improved over the tawdry trailer homes of yesteryear. And many a new mobile home park, the new term for such neighborhoods, is as attractive as a typical new residential area.

New house developments in a growing number of residential areas are being built with mobile-home houses, and a growing number of them are designed and built like conventional houses. An attractive mobile home is pictured in Figure 8.1. They're made with conventional wood-siding walls, asphalt shingle roofs and conventional windows and doors. Virtually everything inside conforms to standard home-building practices. And they are located on permanent foundations. The big difference, however, is that these "mobile" homes are priced sharply lower than conventional houses.

Two of these new breed housing developments were mentioned in Chapter 1. One significant one, a pace-setting development, is Lake Mountain Estates, overlooking Lake Mead in

Figure 8.1 *Here is an example of one of six custom floor plans and exterior elevations designed by Fleetwood Homes and architect Lou Vallaescusa for Haley Ranch Estates. All six plans have three bedrooms and two full baths and are prepared at the factory to accept the two-car garage and entrance features. This model contains 1,129 square-feet of living space in addition to the 400-square-foot garage. Attractive mobile homes like this can hold their heads high in many a suburban neighborhood. This example appears more like a middle-income suburban neighborhood than a California development for low-income families. In short, reasonable, attractive mobile homes can be enjoyed at affordable prices for many who can't afford conventional houses. Photo courtesy of Manufactured Housing Institute. Floor plan courtesy of Fleetwood Homes, Riverside, Calif.*

Boulder City, Nevada, some 25 miles from Las Vegas. This is an area where nearby luxury houses at the time were selling for $125,000 and up, according to *Housing* magazine, a trade journal.

The houses in Lake Mountain Estates, basically double and triple-wide mobiles, a few years ago sold for $39,000 up to $85,000, including land. Each house is built on a permanent foundation, with garage and landscaping, and the cost of the land accounted for 30 to 35 percent of the house prices.

One couple nearby seized the opportunity to make a short move for a big profit. They sold their $175,000 conventional house and bought one of the "mobiles" in Lake Mountain Estates for $68,000. The new house is hardly a come-down. It is roomy and satisfactory for considerably less money.

The ability of mobile-home manufacturers to make attractive houses at sharply reduced prices could be significant for many homebuyers. The only other houses close to meeting their prices are modulars. Mobile-home makers are also using their mass-production techniques to turn out "sectional" or conventional houses that meet building codes and are financed by conventional home-loan mortgages. Mobile homes also are obtainable for individual homebuyers who want houses on their own lots.

It should be mentioned that the higher-quality mobile homes may represent only a minority of all mobile homes. Unfortunately, too many mobiles are still losers in the looks department. But, 300 hitters are not numerous in the big leagues, either. It's easier, however, to upgrade mobile homes, so the number of good ones that become full-fledged members of residential America should increase. They could leap forward in popularity, considering the big savings that they offer.

■ THE ADVANTAGES ■

Mobile homes shine in the following ways:

- Their cost, minus land, is roughly half the price of conventional stickbuilt houses. As mentioned earlier, average prices for new stickbuilt houses recently, less land, ranged from $46 to $50 a square foot.

- Built to order, mobile homes can be delivered and ready to move into (completely furnished, if desired) in as little as six weeks from the time of order, and sometimes faster. That compares with at least three to six months for a stickbuilt house to be ready.

- All mobile homes built after June 1976 must conform to FHA standards for construction, fire and electrical safety. All must be equipped with emergency exits, such as pop-out windows, and smoke detectors.

- Interior and exterior maintenance is minimal. Some mobiles have specially treated exterior walls that need only to be washed with detergent or antioxidant.

- Most mobiles are built in units 12 and 14 feet wide, and up to 75 feet long. Some are built as "left-" and "right-hand" units that are bolted together at the home site. Together, the two section units provide up to 2,200 square feet of living space.

- Mobiles are offered with different floor plans, a number of which can be modified to suit individual needs. These include new H and U plans that are called *tri-wides*. They're made with two-section mobile homes separated by a central room in the middle (H plan) or at one end (U plan).

    Add-on sections can provide extra floor space as well as variety to a mobile-home plan. You can choose from a trio of them. The *tip-out* is mainly an alcove, usually 4 to 5 feet deep and up to 12 feet long. It folds, accordion style, into the mobile-home section for delivery, is pulled out to its full-size at the site. The *slide-out* (also called *pull-out*) is similar but larger, thus more spacious.

    There is also the *tag-out*, in effect, an additional room. It's available in varied lengths, 32 feet being very common. The tag-out is more flexible in that it usually can be bought later, while tip-outs and slide-outs usually must be ordered when you buy the mobile home.

- Some mobile home parks are set amid tree-lined streets and have social activity centers and swimming pools. Some are near golf courses. Although their mobile-home units are placed comparatively close together—on lots of less than a quarter acre—privacy is enjoyed by landscaping, shrubbery and fencing. Roughly half of all mobile homes are located in parks and subdivisions; the other half are on private lots. Some parks are for "adults only," with one person in a couple required to be at least 52 years old, thus assuring peace and quiet for those who are bothered by children. That's not fair to families with children, but fortunately more and more mobile home parks are for young families.

- Higher quality mobile homes, especially those located on permanent foundations, do not depreciate markedly. Some go up in value. This trend has been accelerated by the development of parks of condominium mobile homes.

Figure 8.2 *Manufactured by Fleetwood Homes. Photo courtesy of Manufactured Housing Institute.*

- Most mobile homes continue to be financed with personal loan contracts like auto loans. If a mobile home meets certain specifications for size and construction set by the FHA and the VA, it can qualify for the FHA- or VA-guaranteed mortgage loan used for conventional houses. This can mean a low down payment, as well as a lower interest rate.

■ PRICES ■

In recent years, the average price of a mobile home has ranged from $20 to $25 a square foot of floor area. Thus, a 12-foot-wide unit, 70 feet long, costs as little as $16,800. A 14-foot-wide unit, 70-feet long, as little as $19,600. These prices vary, of course, according to manufacturer, type, model, etc.

Double wides sold for twice as much, depending on size in total enclosed floor space. For example, a large mobile home with three or four bedrooms and up to 2,000 square feet of living space sold for $40,000 and up. The cost for a conventional stickbuilt house of the same size was $80,000 to $100,000, depending on location and excluding land.

Another 15 percent of the price of a mobile home must be added to cover the *set-up charge*. That's for tying down the home (storm holders, etc.) and such things as skirting, porch steps and minor landscaping. Sometimes a thousand dollars or more can be saved by ordering a barebones, or unfurnished, mobile home. Not everyone wants the furnishings, including pictures on the walls, that usually come with the typical unit. You provide your own furniture.

In addition, the typical furnishings provided with most mobile homes are not known for quality. They are more like the low common denominator products and materials provided in typical stickbuilt development houses.

Also consider the cost of the land, as with any other house. If you put a mobile on your own land, the total land cost must include the cost of excavation, foundation, paving and utilities, as well as the raw-land cost. If you move into a mobile home park, you will generally pay a monthly ground rental fee.

■   SHOPPING AND BUYING TIPS   ■

A good way to shop the market and see many of the different mobile homes available all in one shot, is to visit a trade show. You can see the whole spectrum. Shows are held regularly in nearly every part of the country. A local mobile-home dealer can tell you where and when the nearest ones to you are held.

The next best eye-opener is to visit mobile-home dealers. Visit at least a few. Before you buy, shopping around is essential not just to save money but also to help you learn about special features to have, and on the other side, not to have. You can save a lot by avoiding unnecessary extras that some dealers encourage you to get.

A dealer may say, for example, "Gosh, as long as you folks are here, take a look at a real beauty—came in just last week. It's hooked up and, why, you could move in tomorrow!" The unit the dealer shows is often loaded with what the trade calls flash, or more gimmicks and useless accessories than the jewelry counter at the five-and-dime store. The list price of every one is included in the total price for the mobile home. Such items include stained wood wine racks, flashy chandeliers, fancy lamps, as well as pictures on the walls. The price of each is tacked on to the price of the house, unless you put your foot down and say no. Request a breakdown of everything you're being charged for, and cross out what you don't need. That can save you money.

Before buying a mobile home, check on the dealer by calling the Better Business Bureau and a local bank that finances mobile homes. Obviously, the more money at stake, the more urgently you need to make such queries. Speak up now so that you can avoid potentially larger problems later.

If you're a buyer who plans to move into a mobile home park, there's a good way to determine if you're headed for a congenial community or a Pandora's box: *Talk to mobile owners who live there.* Ring some doorbells and ask the owners a few questions. Explain that you're thinking of moving in, and often it's like turning on a faucet: Facts about the area will pour out.

Ask specifically what's good and what's not good about the area and the landlord. Were promised services, like trash pickup, not provided? Are repairs made promptly? How many ground rent increases have there been? Is the park clean, safe and quiet?

If you plan to put a mobile home on a private lot, check with the local planning board and building inspector. Many places flatly ban mobile homes. Other places permit them, but local enforcement officials can make it tough before approval is given. Checking ahead of time is essential.

■ CHECKING THE QUALITY OF MOBILE HOMES ■ BEFORE BUYING

You can get an "X-ray view" of the anatomy of mobile homes by visiting a factory to see how they're made. You'll see the different kinds of products and materials that make up the bones and body, the various organs, how the skin, including insulation, is put on, how the kitchen and bath are made, how carpeting and other furnishings are installed and so on. That anatomical course in mobile-home construction can be eye-opening. Mobile homes are seldom shipped more than 250 or so miles from the factory, so don't waste time considering models made farther away.

■ CONSTRUCTION QUALITY ■

Every mobile home made after June 15, 1976, Magna Charta day for mobile homes, must conform to the structural standards of the U.S. Department of Housing and Urban Development (HUD); a notice stating this should be on any mobile home you buy. Any dealer can show it to you.

The standards not only specify the minimum requirements for the construction of floors, walls, roof, insulation and other such structural shell items; they also call for additional such needs. Examples include two exterior doors remote from each other; at least one egress window in each sleeping room, i.e., a window that a person can escape from in an emergency; smoke detectors wired to the electrical system with audio alarms outside each bedroom area; a tie-down system of cable straps that will make the unit hurricane-safe by anchoring it to the ground; and an electric wiring system that conforms to the National Electrical Code C-1, which is the same code used for conventional houses.

Mobile homes are now considerably less of a fire hazard than formerly when many inflammable plastics, including vinyl materials, were used in them. Because plastics are made from petroleum, increases in the price of crude oil (petroleum) can make these synthetics costly. As a result, many makers have returned to using wood paneling, plasterboard interiors and related materials for mobile homes.

■ BUYING A HIGH-QUALITY MOBILE HOME ■

This can be summed up in one sentence: Buy a top-of-the-line model. I mentioned earlier that marginal or low-quality products are commonly used in run-of-the-mill mobile homes. These same lowest-cost mobile homes can still display the seal showing compliance with the government's national standards for two reasons.

For one, the HUD standards, like any other building code, do not cover everything that goes into a house. It covers only those parts of the structure that can affect the health and safety of people. For example, the HUD rules specify the minimum lumber size to make the floor, walls and roof safe and strong enough at all times. But they say nothing about the kind of interior wall paneling, kitchen countertops or bathroom fixtures, among other things, that are necessary to retain their good looks, are easy to keep clean, require little upkeep and service and will not wear out quickly. These features depend on the quality of such building materials and products, but they have little or nothing to do with health and safety. Therefore, they are not covered by HUD's rules.

In similar fashion, a heating furnace must be strong and safe and not be a fire hazard. But how well it is made for low fuel consumption, maintenance-free operation and long life—all having to do with good quality—are also matters not covered by the HUD standard or, again, by any building code that regulates house construction.

The second reason is that the HUD standard, a very good thing nonetheless, is still no more than a set of floor, or *minimum*, requirements for safety and health. If you want a mobile home that is better than minimum, obviously you must get one that is designed and made better than what is just necessary to pass minimum standards. This principle also applies to nearly all other kinds of factory and stickbuilt houses.

In short, the typical mobile home that meets the government's mobile-home standards is an acceptable product, but if you want a really good, if not top-notch, home, you must aim higher. That's to get a mobile home that will provide easier maintenance, lower upkeep, lower-than-usual monthly energy bills, good looks that remain for a long time, plus a few other things that make the difference between dining with beer and, instead, imbibing a good wine.

To get a first-rate mobile home, step up to a manufacturer's high-quality or top-of-the-line model. It's as simple as that. Of course, you will pay more. But the extra price may be less than you think. Some makers make at least two kinds of mobile homes. The first is their standard model that meets the HUD national standards. It may be a good home but still a bottom-of-the-line mobile, designed to be sold at the lowest possible price. The second is their so-called "quality" model.

A top-of-the-line mobile home is better because of better design, construction and workmanship. Compared with the standard, lowest-priced mobile home, it has thicker and better wall paneling, mitered trim, 2" × 4" wall studs instead of the usual 2" × 3" (which may not be visible but which you can tell by a few raps on the wall), better carpeting with good underlayment; larger, better water heater; better furnace; and, on the outside, long-life walls, rather than the cheap siding found on the lowest-cost mobiles.

Manufacturers of high-quality mobile homes include Dual-wide Homes, New Yorker Homes, Ramada and Skyline. Remember, though, that like other products, including cars and appliances, some manufacturers make both low-priced, lowest-allowable-quality products and much better-made models of the same product.

■ THE WARRANTY ■

Manufacturers sell mobiles with full or limited warranties of up to two years. Some cover only the structure and such items as wiring and plumbing. Others cover the appliances, including the furnace and hot water heater, dishwasher, clothes washer and dryer. If a product breaks down during the warranty period, the manufacturer provides service and repairs through the dealer you bought the unit from.

■ BUYING A USED MOBILE HOME ■

Buying a used mobile home is like buying a used car or an old house. If you shop carefully, you can often find an excellent one at good savings. Let down your guard and you can end up with a lemon. Inspect it carefully and be sure it is in good condition. Hire an expert to inspect it for you. The small fee for this can be worth it. To find an expert, ask people who fix and service mobile homes, or a banker who finances them.

Buying a used mobile can be better than buying a used house because used mobiles often cost a lot less than new ones. A used regular house, on the other hand, generally costs almost as much as a new house, even though the condition of the used house has deteriorated. That's often because the value of the land under the house has increased.

Here are tips when you inspect a used mobile home for sale: Take along a rubber ball, and place it in the center of the kitchen and bathroom floors. If it rolls to a corner, the mobile may need leveling, or the chassis may be sagging, which could lead to

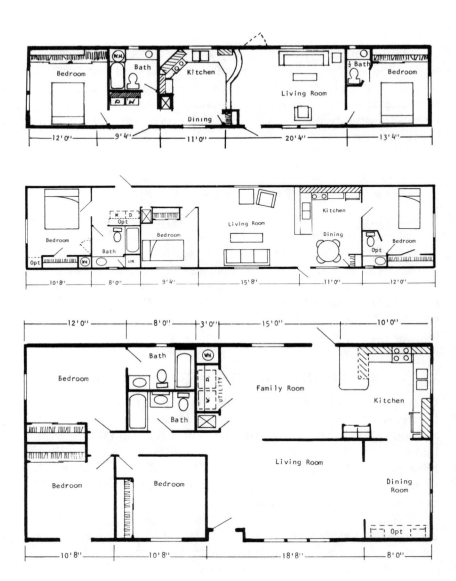

plumbing problems. Also take a small light lamp to check all wall sockets. Test *all* appliances, including the smoke detectors. Don't worry that the dealer may think you're too cautious. Look at it this way: It will be obvious that you're not an amateur.

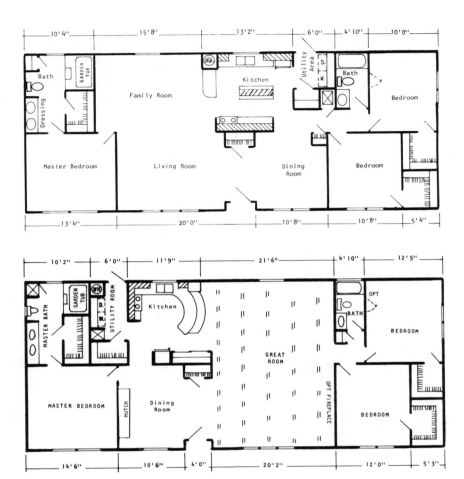

Figure 8.3 *Mobile home plans start with a basic section up to 70 feet or so long. Some manufacturers also provide optional sections with one or more rooms that can be added at right angles to the basic house.*

■ FINANCING A MOBILE HOME ■

The easiest way to finance a mobile home is through the dealer you buy from, but unfortunately that's usually the most expensive way, too. You can save hundreds and often several thousands of dollars if you shop for financing. The best loan is an FHA-insured one; if you're a veteran, a VA loan is an excellent choice, but obtaining one of these can take time and perseverance.

You can qualify for the best financing deal if your mobile home has a foundation, like a regular house. Then you often can get a regular house mortgage loan at the same down payment, repayment schedule and interest rate that is used for regular house mortgage loans. A regular mortgage loan is unquestionably the loan to get for a mobile home anchored to a regular foundation. It's obtained from many of the same banks, savings and loan associations and other lenders who offer regular house mortgage loans.

Financing a conventional mobile home tied to a mobile pad and not anchored to a foundation costs more because it requires the same kind of installment loan used for financing cars. The down payment required ranges from nothing down for a veteran buying with a VA-guaranteed loan, up to about 25 percent down.

The monthly payments depend of course on three variables: the price of the mobile you're buying and thus the size of the principal to be repaid; the interest rate charged; and the length of time to repay it. The longer the repayment period, the more you can stretch out your monthly payments and the lower each monthly payment. But you pay for that privilege by paying more interest over the years. The repayment period can range from a short 5 to 10 years, up to 30 years for a mobile home on a permanent foundation. The terms, including interest rates, vary. You must shop for the best terms.

If you obtain an FHA- or VA-guaranteed loan, the interest rate can be less and over the years it can add up to quite a few dollars saved. FHA and VA loans are obtained from private banks and other lenders, and they can offer other advantages, such as a lower down payment. FHA and VA loans are guaranteed by the government, so there's less risk to the lender and therefore lower cost (reduced interest rate) for the borrower (the mobile-home buyer). Unfortunately, obtaining an FHA or VA loan may involve time-consuming red tape. But it's a small price to pay for the dollar savings they offer.

No matter what kind of financing you seek, the importance of shopping for a good loan at the lowest cost cannot be overstated. You will generally save by obtaining your own loan direct from a lender, rather than financing the deal with your friendly mobile-home dealer who will be delighted to handle the details for you. It's convenient, all right, but it can also cost you extra money. After all, the dealer must do extra work, so why shouldn't he or she be paid extra?

How To Buy
a Thoroughbred
Manufactured House:
Judging Design

Most of us can spot an attractive person at a glance, but for unaccountable reasons we are taste-blind when it comes to houses. Having money makes little difference. Many houses in the richest suburbs have no more style than a neon sign.

In short, they lack good design. Don't shrug off the word *design*. It may sound highfalutin, but it goes deeper than what you see when you first view a house.

Besides being appealing to the eyes, a well-designed house— factory-made or not—fits well on its site, catching loads of bright warm sun in winter and thus lowering winter heating bills. The same house also knows how to brush off the hot sun in summer and thus, lower cooling bills; or, without air conditioning, it's cooler in summer.

Its interior floor plan and room designs make it easy, convenient and a sheer pleasure to live in. It's built of good-quality construction, which means that it's easy to keep clean and maintain and its cost of upkeep is low. The payoff is that a truly well-designed house maintains high resale value over the years. Though many houses have increased in value in recent years, the value of some has risen much more than others.

Witness, for example, the high value put today on the best colonial, federal and other traditional houses of yesteryear. Perhaps most of all, the highest prices are paid today for the best contemporary twentieth-century houses designed by top architects like Frank Lloyd Wright.

The same design principles that make such houses good apply to any house that you buy. Here are the basic things to know when you shop for a manufactured house: good style and appearance, house-to-site relationship, good floor plan and room design and good-quality construction. See *How To Avoid the Ten Biggest Homebuying Traps,* (© A. M. Watkins; published by Real Estate Education Company) for more detail.

■ THE ESSENCE OF HANDSOME LOOKS ■

The key is that a good house has form and style. Its parts fit together in the right proportion. They form a coherent whole; there are no jarring notes. The facade is clean and simple. It is not broken up with a banana-split mishmash of different materials, plus redundant shutters on the windows.

Here are other points to avoid when you look at factory house brochures and photographs: The walls should be neat and straightforward and not jut out here and there for no reason. The roof should sweep across the length and breadth of a house also with no unnecessary broken lines and changes. Breaking up the sweep of the walls and roof of a house with jogs and turns is supposed to add variety and interest, but usually it adds chaos.

Notice that in well-designed houses—those designed by architects and shown in magazines, for example—the tops of the doors and windows almost always line up across the facade. When the opposite occurs, with doors and windows located at different levels as if they were thrown into the wall willy-nilly, the house looks like scrambled eggs. It's out of scale. That's one of the many subtle design blemishes that can detract from resale value.

Watch out for gingerbread, which may be fine in Hansel and Gretel but not so for a house. Adding a lot of unnecessary clutter and doodads to a house, like iron grilles and unnecessary shutters, is like piling cheap jewelry over a flashy dress. It's out of place. Shutters and grillwork may be appropriate in an authentic Georgian Victorian house, but that's something else again. Figures 9.1 to 9.4 are examples of well-designed manufactured homes.

Architects John L. Schmidt, Walter H. Lewis, and Harold Bennett Olin wrote an excellent little discourse on good house design and appearance called *Construction Lending Guide: A Handbook of Homebuilding Design and Construction,* published by the United States Savings and Loan League. Here are some observations that are still valid and useful today:

Exterior Appearance

Pleasing appearance is no accident. Careful study and organization are necessary to anticipate how a house will appear in finished form. The appreciation of a well-designed building is based on recognition and evaluation of the following points.

Figure 9.1 *Two-story colonial house is designed for versatile expansion without violating its traditional architecture. It can come with or without the addition on the left for living purposes or as a garage, or both. The attic may be used for storage or turned into living space. The Fairfax II model. © Nationwide Homes, Inc., 1994. All rights reserved.*

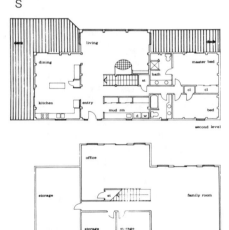

Figure 9.2 *This contemporary house located in a cold northern climate offers excellent design for year-round comfort and livability. Facing south, it's large window areas drink in sunlight and warmth in winter, and the broad outdoor deck provides ready access to the outdoors in summer. All that with a setting designed for a king. Scott House. From* House Warming, *by Susan Aulisi and Doug McGilvary. © 1983. Published by Adirondack Alternate Energy, Edinburgh, NY. Reprinted with permission.*

Proper Proportions

There are basic combinations of shape and mass that result in balanced building proportions. Portions of a building can be out of balance, just as a scale can be tilted. In traditional styling, the proportions of structures and the elements within the design have been refined through many years of study. Roof slopes, overhangs, window shapes, and sizes have all been carefully considered to fit with one another. In today's typical house design (in attempting to achieve the charm of traditional styling) familiar elements are often used without exercising proper care for achieving pleasing proportions.

Visual Organization

A house is a complex arrangement of parts and pieces. Success in exterior design rests in large part on the visual continuity of these elements, which should be related in shape, form and arrangement. Visual organization is the assembling of the parts and pieces with these relationships in mind.

Material Usage, Textures

Materials should be selected for uses appropriate to their capabilities. The elements of a house should be built of materials capable of performing satisfactorily, both initially and over the years.

The visual response aroused by various materials differs greatly. For example, the smooth, "cold" flatness of porcelain-enamel steel panels affects a viewer very differently from a rough, nubby stone wall of rich "warmth." The texture of materials is extremely important in the design of houses and in the selection of materials to be used.

In general, the number of textures selected should be held to a minimum; one type of masonry, one type of wood, or one siding texture, and one neutral "panel" surface per house. Contrasts can be used very successfully, just as a man can be well-dressed with a coat and trousers of different texture. The well-dressed man, however, and the well-dressed house do not wear many varying materials at the same time.

Figure 9.3 *Short of a spectacular view in a million-dollar house, few things can add glamour and excitement better than a cathedral ceiling and skylights. They make a house feel cheerful and open with the interior rooms basking in sun and light that floods into the house. You'll never regret them, assuming that steps are taken to reduce the heat entry in summer, as reported in this chapter. Left: Habitat/American Barn Corp. Below: Yankee Barn Homes, Inc. Reprinted with permission.*

Scale

Scale is the relationship of design elements to the human being. One's visual sense depends in great part on scale relationships in judging distances, sizes and proportions. The size of a door in a house facade can be "in scale," that is, proportioned agreeably to the human being and to the rest of the house; or it can be "out of scale," that is, not properly related to the human figure, overpowering or diminutive in the entire design.

Simplicity and Restraint

To simplify is to refine. In housing, the simplest, most basic designs are the hardest to achieve but simple visual elements are the most pleasing. The attempt to make a house appear more expensive by cheap imitation of expensive items can be disastrous.

Scrollwork and carpentry bric-a-brac can result in design chaos. Such an approach is often based on using many unrelated elements in an effort to develop curb appeal. A storm door with a pelican scroll, a checkerboard garage door, slanted posts at the entranceway, diamond-shaped windows and other parts and pieces having no design continuity detract from appearance and result in a modest house looking cheaper instead of costlier.

The most successful approach is one of restraint. Generally, the simply stated house design is the handsomest. Restraint and sophistication go hand in hand. An opulence and over-decoration are more often than not annoying and disturbing. The simplest designs are the most agreeable in the long run.

Color

Color is a highly potent factor in the design of a group of houses taken as a whole. In this respect, color coordination is a major way to strengthen that pleasing individuality from house to house, the objective of good subdivision design. Color is actually so powerful that it can make a cracker-box house look attractive or a generally well-designed house look repulsive. It all depends on the skill with which color is used. When a large group of houses is involved, the overall effect of color is a major concern. The cluttered, disorganized look of the

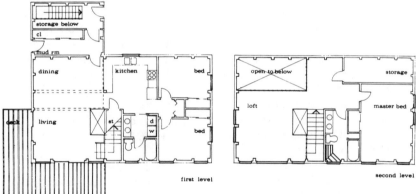

Figure 9.4 *This 2,000 square foot Saltbox is designed for year-round comfort in a cold climate at surprisingly low cost. Located in upstate New York, it faces south to let the considerably warm sun into the house in winter, and it's built with thick thermal insulation, insulating wood sheathing and insulating window glass. Auxiliary heating is provided by a stove that burns as little as one cord of wood for full winter heating, according to the manufacturer. A 175-foot run of underground pipe provides chilled water for summer cooling. Roof overhangs shade the second-story window glass, which reduces the interior cooling load in summer. Framing is rough-sawn pine timber frame. Adirondack Alternate Energy. Photo of King house by Mark Antam. From* House Warming, *by Susan Aulisi and Doug McGilvary. Published by Adirondack Alternate Energy, Edinburgh, NY.*

average subdivision of low-to-moderate-priced houses (or even more expensive ones) is due largely to lack of color coordination. Clashing roofs, anemic body colors, misplaced accent colors—all these result from the short-sighted practice of giving the buyer too much latitude in selecting exterior color.

The All-Around Look

Unfortunately, most houses are designed like a Hollywood set. Some concern is evidenced over the appearance of the street facade, but often the side and rear elevation are totally neglected. A well-designed house, like a piece of sculpture, should be handsome when viewed from any vantage point.

A Few Words about Style

A well-known architect, Alden Dow, FAIA, puts it simply: "Style is a result, it can never be an objective. When style itself becomes the objective, nothing results but a copy."

What determines style? The shape and character, or style, of a house should be determined by the plan, the site, methods and materials of construction, and by the budget. A particular set of circumstances, worked upon by the design process, logically will lead to a particular set of building shapes or appearance. It might be correct to say that the well-designed house is styleless, since no forcing of the solution has been made by adapting it to the framework of a "traditional" scheme. Traditional styles are, of course, in predominance and undoubtedly will remain so for many years. But there are other styles to consider.

Here are four terms often discussed in describing other than traditional architecture: modern, modernistic, contemporary, and futuristic.

A modern house is one built of up-to-date materials: it has most of the current electrical and mechanical gadgetry in place and may exhibit itself as a simplified expression of any of the whole bag of traditional styles. It is harmless in design—not bad perhaps—but not great architecture.

A modernistic house is a poorly designed "jazzy" modern house. Often it is an attempt at being unusual, generally is designed by a contractor or individual and is usually a collection of pieces (perhaps a flat roof or a butterfly roof, round windows, slanted posts, big "picture-windows") with no integration of parts into a carefully studied design.

A contemporary house generally is one done by an architect and grows in its design from the consideration of beauty, function and site. The market confuses good contemporary design with modernistic and fails to perceive the great difference between the two. Contemporary design is not faddish, or subject to being "in" today, "out" tomorrow. On the contrary, it's extremely rare, especially in lower-cost houses.

A futuristic house is somewhat experimental in nature. New products or methods may be tried or tested, and generally the futuristic house attempts to present an image of tomorrow's house. It may be, and usually is, a properly conceived design, but its importance on the market is inconsequential.

Poorly designed modernistic houses invariably will be penalized by the market, but an honestly conceived contemporary home, large or small, is of lasting value. Little research is necessary to recognize that a fine piece of architecture appreciates in value and appeal. Certainly the demand far exceeds the small supply.

How To Test the Floor Plan and Other Rooms

Some people think that meat and potatoes is the only meal to dine on: They don't know about or prefer any other meals.

Similarly, many people don't realize that a floor plan is more than a few rooms connected in one way or another. Then they wonder why living in a house with a sick plan can drive them up a wall. See Figure 10.1.

That's the difference between a factory house with a poor plan and one with a good plan, including good interior room design and things like good "zoning." These can make an enormous difference in the pleasure and sheer enjoyment that you get—or don't get—from a house. Here is what to know about them when you shop.

The key to a good floor plan is that it permits good circulation and traffic flow from room to room and also in and out of a house. Like highway traffic, you want to avoid snags, tie-ups and jams. Apply the following tests to each plan. But also be flexible, especially if you're buying a mobile home or other compact house where the design and the floor plan in particular sometimes must be compromised a bit for economy reasons. On the other hand, a good number of manufacturers will vary their

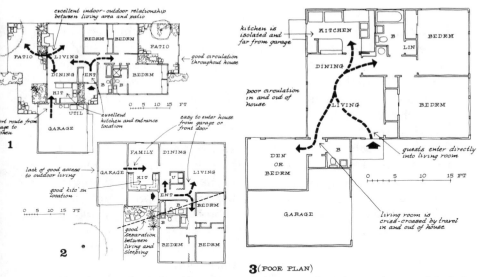

Figure 10.1 *Floor plans show important features to have in your house and typical mistakes to avoid. © A. M. Watkins.*

standard floor plan for you on request and often with little or no extra charge.

1. *The main entrance*, the front door, should funnel people, mostly visitors, directly to the living room. An entrance foyer is highly recommended for receiving guests. A coat closet nearby is virtually essential. The main entrance should be quickly and easily accessible from the driveway and street in front. It should also be quickly accessible from the rooms inside, where you are likely to be when the doorbell rings, and especially from the kitchen. The kitchen-to-front-door route is one of the most frequently used paths. A foyer is also important as a buffer or transfer chamber to keep howling winds, snow and rain from blowing into the heart of a house every time someone comes in the front door.

2. *A separate family entrance*, ordinarily a back or side door, should lead directly into the kitchen area. This is the door most used by a family itself, especially children. A proper location is important to permit swift unloading of groceries,

for example. It should also be located so that children can travel in and out easily and can quickly get to where they're going inside the house (such as a nearby bathroom). The route from the car to this entrance should be sheltered from rain and from snow and ice in a cold climate. But the route from it through the kitchen should not run smack through the kitchen working area.

3. *The living room* should have a dead-end location for the reasons noted earlier plus a few others. It should not be a main route for everybody's travel around the house. Only then can you entertain guests in peace or just read or watch television without being continually disturbed by others walking through. Sometimes one end wall of the living room serves as a traffic lane; in effect, it's a hallway. That's all right if it happens to work in a particular house. Sometimes, though, a screen or half-wall may be necessary between it and the heart of the living room.

4. *The room arrangement* should be designed so that you can go from any room in the house to any other without going through a third room except possibly the dining room. Direct access to a bathroom from any room is particularly important. Yet in some houses this rule is violated to the consternation of its occupants, and there are even houses in which access to a bedroom is possible only through a bathroom! This is unpardonable, no matter what kind of factory house you may buy. If the bathroom is occupied, a person is trapped in the bedroom like a prisoner, unable to get out (unless he doesn't mind going out a window).

5. *The kitchen* should have a central location. It should not be located way out in a left-field corner of the house. In the kitchen one should be close to the front door, should be able to oversee children playing in the family room, say, or outside, and should be able to get to the dining room, the living room, or the terrace without long hikes back and forth. That's particularly important when entertaining.

6. *The main travel routes* between the house and the outdoor living areas—patio, terrace, or porch—should be short and direct. Can guests as well as family members go in and out

easily? Is the outdoor area that you use most during pleasant weather easily accessible from the house? If it is, it will be used often. If not, you'll find it neglected and your family involuntarily depriving itself of outdoor-living benefits.

Those are the characteristics of a good floor plan. They're not always easy to get, since making a really efficient floor plan is tough to do in the design of a house. The importance of some of the individual tests will, of course, vary from family to family, depending on your own living habits and the activities you consider most important.

If you like to spend a lot of time outside the house, for example, you may place high importance on efficient access to the outdoors. If you entertain often, the design and location of the dining room and living room for entertaining are vital for successful social events. The way you live therefore should be taken sharply into account so that your house will simplify daily living activities and make life a lot more pleasant.

■ INTERIOR ZONING ■

Interior zoning is concerned with the logical arrangements of the rooms inside the house. Ideally, every house should have three clearcut zones to accommodate the three main kinds of activities: living, sleeping and working. The living zone embraces the living, dining and family rooms, in which you engage in most activities other than working and sleeping. The work zone embraces the kitchen, laundry and perhaps a workshop, where obvious, if not unavoidable, work of one kind or another goes on. The sleeping zone embraces the bedrooms. Each zone should be separate from the other. The two-story house provides natural zoning between the bedrooms upstairs and the other rooms downstairs with natural benefits.

Regardless of the kind of house, a buffer wall or other such separation is essential between the bedrooms and the other

two zones, if for no other reason than to permit you to entertain guests without disturbing children at study or in bed at
night. The kitchen and work zone should be separate from the
living area. Can dishes be left stacked and unwashed there
without being seen by guests in the living room? Can laundry
be left unfinished but out of view when visitors call unexpect-
edly (or even when they are expected)? The answers should be Yes.
These type of questions will tell you if a house plan has
good zoning.

■   THE KITCHEN   ■

The kitchen deserves top-priority attention. A homemaker usually spends more work time there than in any other single room. It
also represents a high-cost part of a house (because of its
heavy-equipment concentration). Its cost can run half as much
again as the average square-foot cost of a typical house. The
kitchen more than any other room also can influence the resale
value of your house. It is clearly important, and its design
elements should be explored in some detail.

A central location is the first requisite, as noted earlier. The
kitchen also rates a good exposure in relation to the sun. The
same principles apply for overall orientation of a house as those
in Chapter 13. The best kitchen exposure is one with windows on
the southeast; next best is south. That will let most bright light
and sunshine flood in during the day for at least the eight months
from September to April. It will mean a bright, airy kitchen most
of the time when you want it, yet the same exposure is easy to
shade on hot summer days. With a factory house, this of course
means that the house be tailored for its lot, or vice versa.

A kitchen facing east gets sun in the morning, but that's
about all. One facing west gets little or no sun except in the
afternoon, and in summer it will get hit with hot afternoon sun.
A northern exposure is darkest and gloomiest of all, receiving
the least sun and light the year around. The same exposure
principles also apply to a dining room or other area that is used
for most meals.

Kitchen Work Triangle

The heart of a kitchen is its "work triangle," the arrangement of the refrigerator, sink and range in relation to each other. The entire process of efficiently preparing and cooking foods hinges on a good work triangle. From the refrigerator to sink to range should form a triangle with a total perimeter of at least 12 to 15 feet, but no more than 22 feet, according to research at Cornell University's renowned kitchen laboratory. The appliances should be in that order to conform with the natural sequence of cooking.

Plenty of countertop space around the triangle is also a must. The University of Illinois Small Homes Council recommends these minimum standards: at least 4½ feet of countertop length on the open-door side of the refrigerator between the refrigerator and the sink; 3½ to 4 feet of countertop length between the sink and range; and at least 2 feet of countertop on the other side of the range. That adds up to a minimum of at least 10 feet of countertop length in all. An additional 2 feet of countertop is desirable, if not essential, at or near the range as a last-step serving center, where food is put on plates before being taken to the table. If the refrigerator, sink or range is separate from the other triangle centers—on a separate wall, for example—extra countertop space should be placed at its side, in addition to the minimum standards just given.

Make sure that the refrigerator door opens the right way—toward the counter between the refrigerator and sink—so food can be conveniently unloaded where you want it. The wrong-door refrigerator is a common flaw. A separate wall oven can go almost anywhere. Once it's loaded, it can usually be turned on without attention until the bell rings. A location near the range is not essential, but because of its heat, it should not be flush next to the refrigerator.

Any ample kitchen core and work triangle usually require a space at least 8 feet by 12 feet (96 square feet). That's the minimum to look for. With a dishwasher and separate oven, more space is needed. This should be an exclusive self-contained part of the kitchen out of the way of the main traffic routes used by people passing through the kitchen from one part of the house to another.

Kitchen Storage

According to studies at the University of Illinois, a minimum of at least 8½ running feet of wall cabinets and storage shelves is recommended for the kitchen. Another rule calls for at least 20 square feet of interior storage space under the countertop plus at least 10 square feet in wall cabinets. The proper cabinets and shelves should be put where they can house the particular items needed in each part of the kitchen. For example, storage for dishes and pots and pans near the sink and range; storage for working knives, bread box, flour, and other staples near the sink and refrigerator, and so on.

Because kitchen cabinets can run into big money, consider open shelves for certain items. They can be a lot cheaper. If not enough cabinets or shelves are in a house, space should be available against walls or under the countertop to add what you'll need. The quality of cabinets is also important. You'll certainly want attractive cabinets with a rugged, hard finish that is easy to keep clean and will stay attractive over the years. To roll in and out easily, the drawers should have nylon rollers; try them and see. The cabinet hardware and latches should be of good quality.

Fixtures and Appliances

The best kitchen sinks are made of stainless steel or enameled cast iron. Both are easy to keep clean and will retain their good looks over the years. There are also porcelain-on-steel sinks, which may look like cast iron; they are hard to keep clean, chip easily and lose their gloss quickly. Sometimes the material of which it is made will be noted right on it; other times you must ask about it. You'll want a single-lever "one-armed" faucet rather than the old-style double-handle type. (More on faucets in Chapter 11.)

Appliances are largely a matter of preference. Sometimes when buying a factory house the appliances are optional, and you may bring along your own. You should know, however, which ones do or do not come with it. Those that are included should be noted in the sales contract to avoid a common misunderstanding that occurs when people buy houses.

Gas or Electric Range?

This is particularly important because electric cooking costs up to five times more than cooking with gas. The exact extra price paid for electricity depends on the local cost for each in your area. Even if gas rates rise faster in the future than electric rates, gas should remain significantly cheaper for a long time. Gas costs will have to rise by more than 400 percent, which is quite a bit, before they reach the cost level of electric cooking.

The dollar cost of cooking with gas comes to about $5 to $10 a month versus $20 to $30 a month for electricity. Calls to your local utilities get you specific figures on the comparative cost of gas and electric cooking for your house.

In general, you can save about $10 to $20 a month with a gas range, so gas is obviously the more economical choice. An electric range for the kitchen is recommended only when you have a strong personal preference for electricity that offsets paying more —as much as $200 or so more a year—to cook with electricity.

Gas is cheapest of all if it is also used for the house furnace and water heater. Then your gas cost will fall to the lowest rate. That's a result of higher use; generally the more you use, the lower the rate. Similar reduced rates on a step-down schedule also usually apply for electricity; the more used each month, the lower its unit cost. That is often mentioned when electric companies promote the all-electric house.

Your total energy bill each month for electric heat and gas for cooking, water heater and other gas use will often be lower than the cost of electricity for all your energy. The exact savings vary according to local energy rates, which you must figure yourself according to the local rates for each. See Chapter 12 for more on energy.

Final Checks for the Kitchen

Try to visualize the overall kitchen. It should be large enough to hold the table required by your family, or an adequate dining area should be nearby. Some people also like space for a work desk and perhaps a sewing table. The laundry should be nearby, or you may desire space in one part of the kitchen for a washer, dryer and ironing board. A laundry located on the second floor of a two-story house can be a good thing. It not only saves stair-climbing but puts the equipment at the largest source of the wash.

Are electric outlets spaced behind the countertop for convenient use of small appliances? If not, how will you operate a mixer, blender, electric frying pan, toaster and coffee maker? You'll want good lighting from above and light over the full countertop. Finally, you need good ventilation to keep the kitchen free of cooking fumes and odors. A built-in exhaust fan is the least required. It should be located in the wall directly behind and above the range or in the ceiling directly over it. If located elsewhere, its exhaust efficiency will be low. A large range hood with built-in fan is even better. It should exhaust outdoors through a duct. There are also "ventless" hoods equipped only with filters, with the hot air drawn through the filter and spilled back into the kitchen; they do not cool a kitchen.

■ OTHER ROOMS ■

Windows make an enormous difference. They are the biggest single ingredient for making a room cheerful, large and pleasant. They turn a small space into a virtual ballroom.

So look for ample window glass to let in light, air and sunshine, the main reasons for windows. But obviously they should not let in a lot of cold in winter and hot sun in summer. You can have your cake and eat it, too, through careful design and window location. In general, a southern exposure for your windows is best of all, east or west next best, and north is worst of all.

At the same time, nearly every room needs enough unbroken wall area for easy furniture placement. Rooms should be large enough to hold your furniture. Good heating, enough electric outlets and good lighting are also points to check. As for size and location, here are some minimum standards from the University of Illinois Small Homes Council. For pamphlets and further information, contact The Building Research Council, University of Illinois at Urbana-Champaign, 800/336-0616.

- *A living room at least 12' × 20', with at least 10 to 12 feet of unbroken wall for a couch.* Remember, the living room should not be a major highway for traffic through the house, and the front door of the house should not open directly into it.

- *A family room of at least 12' × 16', though 12' × 20' is better.* It should be on the same level as the kitchen and near the kitchen.

- *Bedrooms at least 9' × 11½', with at least 4 square feet of closet space per person.* The bedrooms should have privacy from the rest of the house, and the master bedroom should have built-in privacy from the children's bedrooms. You'll notice that notable custom houses published in architectural magazines show that the master bedroom is located apart from other bedrooms, if not by itself on the other side of the house from children's rooms.

  That's the result of architects designing individual houses to fit the needs of individual families. It's not easy to do in a modest-priced house, and it's not often found in factory-made houses. Still, it sometimes can be achieved by modifying a factory-house plan. Think about it. It can make an excellent feature that you will enjoy.

  I've mentioned that a 12-foot dimension for one side of any room of a house, including living and family room, will provide a satisfactory room. That's also generously ample for a good bedroom. It will satisfy the minimum standards for a good room.

■ COMMON HOUSE TRAPS ■

Here are 22 common little flaws in factory-made as well as other houses. This list also shows how good design embraces the important little things, as well as the big, and that good design involves more than style and good looks.

• No separate entranceway or foyer to receive visitors.

• No opening in the front door, or no window or glass outlook alongside that lets you see who's at the door.

• No roof overhang or similar protection over the front door for shelter from rainy weather.

• No direct access route from the driveway to the kitchen.

• No direct route from outdoors to bathroom so children can come in and out with minimum of bother and mud-tracking.

• Gas, electric and water meters inside the house or in the garage or basement, rather than outside. Outside meters do away with the need to let in meter readers every month.

• Fishbowl picture window in the front of the house, exposing you to every passerby.

• The nightmare driveway that opens out on a blind curve so you cannot see oncoming traffic when backing out. A driveway that slopes up to the street is almost as bad, especially for trapping you hopelessly on a winter morning when your car won't start.

• Isolated garage or carport with no direct access from car to house.

• Accident-inviting doors that open toward the basement stairs.

• Cut-up rooms with windows haphazardly located. Sometimes too many doors make it impossible to arrange furniture.

- Windows in children's rooms that are too low for safety, too high to see out of, and/or too small to get out of in case of fire.

- A hard-to-open window, usually the double-hung type, over the kitchen sink. An easily cranked casement window is usually best here; a sliding window, second best.

- A window over the bathroom tub. This generally causes cold drafts as well as rotted windowsills because of condensation.

- Stage-front bathrooms placed in view of a space like the living room or smack in view at the top of the stairway. Ideally, you should be able to go from any bedroom to the bathroom without being seen from another part of the house.

- Only one bathroom, especially tough on you in a two-story or split-level house.

- No light switches at every room entrance and exit.

- No light or electrical outlet on a porch, patio or terrace.

- No outside light to light up the front path to and from the house.

- Child-trap closets that can't be opened from inside.

- Small closets that are hardly big enough for half your wardrobe. Also watch out for narrow closet doors that keep part of a closet out of reach without a fishing pole, shelves too high for a person of normal height and clothes poles so low that dresses and trousers cannot hang without hitting the floor.

C·H·A·P·T·E·R   11

Getting a Good Bathroom, the Highest-Cost Room

The bathroom rates a chapter of its own because it's the highest-cost room in a house, but also because it must withstand harder use and abuse than any other part of the house. It pays to be sure to get good ones in the factory house you buy.

That means a bathroom that's tough, easy to keep clean and attractive; requires a minimum of maintenance over the years; and will not start looking rundown and shabby in a short time. Knowing how to get a good bathroom is particularly important with a factory house because the bathroom fixtures and other parts often must be provided by the buyer since many manufacturers do not include this part of the house with their house packages.

The location of each bathroom is also important. At least one should be near the bedrooms. If it's the only one in the house, it should be convenient to other rooms as well.

Two or three bathrooms are essential for a family. If an extra bathroom is wanted in a new house, arrange for it when the house is ordered rather than after you move in. It can be installed for a much lower cost at that time than when the house is completed. If that requires more extra money than you can afford, plan ahead for the future location of the additional bathroom you'll need later. Have the main plumbing pipes supplied to it and capped for future use. The stitch-in-time cost to do this can be small and the savings later large when you complete the installation.

A big sales feature in houses is the private bathroom for the master bedroom, but this is not always good. In a two-bathroom house it might be better to have the grown-ups' bathroom outside the master bedroom, where it is accessible to guests. Otherwise guests may be restricted to using the children's bathroom, which is often an embarrassing mess. Free the master bathroom, and the second bath can be given over to the children. Most manufacturers will change the location of a master bathroom on request. This is unnecessary, of course, if a third bath or powder room is available for friends and visitors.

A full bathroom may be as small as 5' × 7', and a half-bath (powder room) as small as 24" × 40" or so. However, the key to adequate bathroom size is not necessarily the dimensions but the number of people who are likely to be using it, particularly during the hectic morning rush hour. The more baths, the smaller the load on each and the less the need for large baths. You can usually tell by sight if a bathroom is large enough to handle two or three children or two adults at once.

Extra bathrooms are not always necessary. Two lavatories, or washbowls, for example, may save you the expense of an additional bathroom. Two of them side by side can provide double-duty and help to solve the morning rush-hour problem. Sometimes a bathroom can be equipped with two toilet compartments, which also may be adequate and less costly than an extra bath. These are ideas for families with children.

■ COMPARTMENT PLAN ■

A whole bathroom for a large family can be compartmentalized, an idea heavily promoted by fixture manufacturers, though not found in many manufactured houses. If desired, ask about getting this in a factory house you buy. Toilets, shower and sometimes the tub are fenced off by partitions, which enable from two to three people to use the bathroom simultaneously with privacy. Partitions, dividers or folding doors may be used. If two toilets are used, each has a private enclosure like a public bathroom. Two washbowls are mandatory; a second tub or shower stall is optional. A compartment bath is equivalent to having two or three bathrooms, but plumbing and construction costs are lower as a result of grouping all the fixtures together within one wall enclosure. A space of at least 8' × 10½' is required to start with; but 10' × 12' is better.

The merits of the compartment bath, however, are open to question. It has received publicity because large fixture manufacturers landed on it as a good way to sell more fixtures—two instead of one at a crack. Merely partitioning off the toilet in a large bath coupled with double washbowls often can serve a family as well at less expense. Or you may do better with a separate second bathroom elsewhere, especially in a large house.

■ Choosing Good Bathroom Fixtures ■

The old traditional fixtures—bathroom sink, toilet and tub—are made of china, steel or cast iron. The newcomers are made of rigid plastic, which are increasingly used in manufactured houses. Here I'll consider the traditional materials first, though they're not always installed in manufactured houses. But if they are available and desirable, it's important to get good-quality ones. Rigid plastic fixtures can be just as good, and sometimes you have no choice. You must take them because they're standard equipment. More about them later.

Traditional washbowls, toilets and tubs come in three quality grades. Like many products in the homebuilding business, they're labeled "good," "better" and "best." But that's not always accurate. What's called "good" is in some cases cheap, low quality that shouldn't be given to dogs.

In order of increasing quality and durability, washbowls are made of *enameled steel,* the bottom-of-the-line; *enameled cast iron,* the middle; and *vitreous china,* the top-of-the-line. A steel bowl is least desirable because it is difficult to fuse a durable enamel finish on steel. In time the finish pops off.

The finish on both steel and cast-iron bowls is porcelain enamel, a form of melted glass. It adheres to cast iron much better than to steel, so it's silly to accept steel. An enameled cast-iron bowl is far more chip-resistant and has a permanent finish. It's especially recommended in a child's bathroom where it can take tough knocks without showing (which is why it's often specified for schools and hospitals).

The vitreous-china bowl, the top-of-the-line, is not necessarily as chip-proof as enameled cast iron, but it's still very tough. It is top quality because of its gleaming finish and handsome looks. It's also more versatile than cast iron because it can be cast into a greater variety of shapes and sizes and costs only a little more than cast iron.

Whichever you choose, don't be cursed with a midget bowl. Some are so small that merely washing your hands will bruise your knuckles. They're also too small for washing your hair or bathing a new baby. Once hooked up, you're stuck with it. Yet the price difference between a luxuriously large 20" × 24" bowl and the small but commonly sold 17" × 19" model is no more than the price of a few steaks.

■ THE BATHTUBS ■

Bathtubs are made of enameled steel or enameled cast iron. They're not made of vitreous china because china can't be molded in large sizes except at prohibitive cost. The enameled steel tub is the cheaper kind, but it's not all that bad, provided that it's not subjected to rough use. It can be installed by one person, an advantage in do-it-yourself installation. However, installing cast-iron tubs requires two people. A cast-iron tub is a better buy because of its durability and superior resistance to chipping. It costs about $100 to $150 more than a steel tub.

When a shiny new tub is first used, people often discover that it's too shallow or small, or both. A typical tub is 30 inches wide, 14 inches deep and 4½ or 5 feet long. So specify a larger size—at least 32 inches wide, 16 inches deep and 5 feet long. That increase may seem small, but it makes a big difference in bathing comfort. It also will mean less splashed water on the floor. Also be sure to get a slip-resistant tub bottom.

To cut costs, fixture makers have cut the depth of their tubs to as low as 12 inches! It's hardly off the floor. Shallow depth is usually what you will get unless you specify a tub at least 16 inches deep. This is essential if you like tub baths and want to avoid wild splashing over the floor with children.

A square tub shape can be interesting if it is large enough and has a seat at one or both ends. People need one at least 4 feet square but often get saddled with a minitub hardly larger than a washbowl.

Bathtubs come in a rainbow range of colors. A colored tub generally costs 5 to 10 percent more than a white tub. Tubs are also available in models designed especially for the person who craves luxury bathing: tubs with body-contoured shapes, reclining-back designs, beveled headrests and, for the true Roman bather, ultradeluxe poollike tubs.

■ TOILETS ■

There are three basic toilets, according to government standards:

1. *The washdown,* which is the aboriginal toilet, is unchanged since the Spanish-American War. It's the bottom-of-the-line model. It needs frequent cleaning and is unsanitary, prone to clogging and noisy. A washdown toilet is easy to spot because the water drains out the front of the bowl. Some building codes prohibit the washdown, and it has been phased out by many manufacturers. But it's still available in the supply channels. Take care to avoid it.
2. *The reverse trap,* the middle-of-the-line model, flushes water out through a rear trap—thus its name. It is cleaner, more sanitary and more efficient than the washdown because of greater water surface, deeper water seal and large-diameter drain passage, which also makes it quieter. There are, however, marked differences among brands. Some have a greater-

than-minimum water surface, larger-than-minimum drains and a better flush mechanism. Their prices vary, depending on brand, quality of flush mechanism and how much a model exceeds the minimum government standards.

3. *The siphon jet* is the quietest and most efficient toilet. Flush action is excellent, because water from the tank is discharged through jets located around the top rim of the bowl. It's also called a "quiet-flush" unit, and it is identified by its one-piece construction and low-slung shape.

There is also the handsome wall-mounted toilet which hangs entirely above the floor. It eliminates the big floor-cleaning problem encountered around a conventional toilet. This kind also can be comparatively quiet in operation if you get the right brand; some wall-hung brands, on the other hand, are noisy. The quiet kinds are identified by their low-slung tank and one-piece construction. A conventional high tank, separate from the bowl, is the tip-off to noisy operation, sometimes as loud and noisy as the cheapest washdown toilet. A wall-hung toilet may require beefing up the wall, but this should not be a problem in a factory house.

Like the floor-mounted quiet-flush toilet, a wall-hung toilet is more expensive than standard toilets. But many people say it is worth the expense.

Like cars, toilets come with optional features that you may like. These include an elongated bowl shape that is usually better and more sanitary than a round bowl, a self-ventilating bowl that is especially good for an interior bath, and the water-saver toilet which uses roughly one-third less water per flush than regular models. If you have high-cost water, this last can much cut monthly water bills since toilet flushes account for a major portion of most families' water use.

■ **THOSE NEW PLASTIC FIXTURES** ■

The new rigid fiberglass and acrylic plastic lavatories, bathtubs and shower stalls are being used in a growing number of factory houses, especially since they're light in weight and therefore mean reduced shipping and handling costs. They can be very good provided that you get well-made ones. They are attractive, tough and long lasting; they're made of the same tough plastic used for boat hulls, which must withstand rugged exposure to water and hard knocks. Plastic units are also warm to the touch, a welcome comfort in winter, and are much lighter in weight than traditional metal and china fixtures. Their light weight can cut installation costs and be a heaven-sent boon for those who build their own house.

A one-piece plastic shower stall and tub can cut bathroom costs in a factory house not only because of their light weight, but also because they provide a hard, waterproof wall at less cost than tile or any other waterproof wall material. A stall for tub or shower is made with integral floor and sidewalls (which elimi-nate leaky grouted joints). The walls have a low-gloss finish that is impervious to alkalis, mold, fungus and household solvents, but an abrasive detergent cleanser should not be used on them.

If you buy a factory house for which the plumbing is installed locally after delivery and plastic fixtures are to be used, be sure to get good-quality plastic ones. Many cheap, shoddy ones are available that are tempting to buy because of their low price. The plumber doing your bathroom installation may easily fall for these. Don't let yourself be a victim.

To protect yourself, specify a brand that meets the stiff design standards of the American National Standards Institute, or ANSI Z 124, 1-1974. A shower unit should meet the ANSI Z 124, 2-1967 standard. Accept only a plastic lavatory made by a well-known company, which will replace it if something goes wrong. Another check is FHA (Federal Housing Administration) acceptance of a manufacturer's unit. Ask about this. (Buying a product that comes with FHA acceptance is a good rule to use with many housing products.)

Plastic fixtures tend to be priced higher than conventional fixtures, but that's offset by lower-cost installation. A good plastic tub-wall unit, for example, may cost more than the lowest-cost enameled steel tub, but no more and maybe less than the same size top-of-the-line cast-iron model. And you don't have to spend more money to cover the surrounding walls.

■ WATER SPIGOTS, FAUCETS ■
AND SHOWER HEADS

Plumbers call these the *fittings* or the *trim*. They are taken for granted by nearly everybody, and we can be cursed with faucets that drip and trim that tarnishes or rusts. Getting faucets that will operate long and well is important because faucets are among the hardest workhorses in houses. They must withstand harder use than almost any other part of a house, with the possible exception of a swinging door in the party room. So know a little about faucets. What follows also applies to faucets for the kitchen and anywhere else you have one.

You can't count on getting good faucets and other trim simply by ordering a good bathroom bowl and tub. Fittings are ordered and shipped separately and are not always made by the fixture manufacturer. Like other parts of the bathroom, faucets are also made in three quality grades: low, high and luxury quality.

The bottom-of-the-line, cheapest faucets and trim are not good because they are usually made with short-lived washers and valves, which is why they drip like a head cold. They also need frequent regrinding of the valve seat.

Bottom-line faucets and trim (e.g., water spouts, hand bars, other metal appurtenances) are also made of a soft alloy— usually zinc with a thin top coat of chrome. They shine in the showroom, but once in use they tarnish as fast as they drip. There are exceptions, but you can generally spot the cheap faucets by their handles, which have two or more spokes radiating out from the center, like a wheel. The better kinds have solid handles, with a ridged circumference for gripping.

Good faucets and trim, the middle-line kind, cost a little more than the cheapest, yet will give high-quality performance. They are made with a good water valve that shuns a rubber washer. Some manufacturers use a tough ceramic disk; others a hard plastic mechanism. Both are usually guaranteed for five to ten years.

If the valve seat does go bad, you merely replace it. That's a key thing to remember: Purchase only faucets that come with replaceable valve seats. These better faucets and trim are also made with solid brass bodies. Visit a plumbing supply show-room and you'll quickly see the difference between well-made brass faucets and the cheap kind. Though made of brass, the good guys have a permanent copper-nickel-chrome finish with a tough protective coating applied over the brass body. This gives a durable finish that doesn't tarnish and doesn't require frequent cleaning.

Their looks still may vary. They offer a wide choice of colors and degree of luster for virtually every decor, for example, a brushed satin finish, polished gold or chromium, or highly polished brass.

Good faucets for bathrooms include single-lever models, similar to those used in kitchens. Almost every brand is made with a replaceable valve. Some are made with a top-notch valve, which costs a few dollars more. One of the best is the Moen single-lever. The main things to check when you buy a single-lever faucet are the length of the guarantee and the expense involved if the valve must be replaced. The style and design of single-lever faucets also vary, but this, of course, is an individual choice.

Stepping up to top-of-the-line, deluxe faucets is not worth the extra money just for extra quality. These high-priced faucets are basically made with the same interior guts, basic valves and construction as the middle-line faucets noted above. The fancy price goes for special styling and appearance, including models with a gold-plated finish. That can cost you as much as $300 more.

Shower Nozzles

A good-quality shower nozzle does not easily clog or corrode and has a flexible ball joint to adjust the spray direction. It should have a volume spray control enabling you to obtain a fine or coarse spray. If you have hard water, a self-cleaning head is another good feature. The cheapest kinds have a rigid head, which cannot be adjusted, and little or no volume control.

Water, like energy, is becoming increasingly scarce and expensive, so a shower nozzle that doesn't waste water may be important. Nozzles can spray as little as three gallons a minute of water, up to two to three times that much spray. That obviously can make a difference in your water bill. So check water ratings, too. And definitely specify an adjustable nozzle that allows you to vary the spray as well as the water rate. An adjustable nozzle with a rating of three to seven gallons a minute is usually satisfactory.

How To Cut
Your Home Energy Bills

There is probably no other aspect of building or buying a house where an ounce of prevention can pay off so well as providing energy-saving measures when the house is built. With one exception, here are the main requirements for saving the most energy in your house. The exception is free solar heat in winter, as described in the next chapter.

To cut energy costs, you simply chop away at the main energy drains in houses. The table on the next page shows the main energy drains in American houses based on figures from the U.S. Department of Energy.

The actual energy bills for individual families can, of course, run higher or lower than the average figures above. On the whole you can save considerable money over the years by using high-efficiency equipment and appliances, as well as being informed on energy issues.

Buying a factory house will give you a head start in the energy-saving department, compared with a stickbuilt house. Though all new houses must conform to the energy codes in most states, some codes are tougher than others. A factory house, however, is generally made to conform with the toughest energy code in a manufacturer's sales area. No matter where you live,

Usage	*Percentage of Energy Output*
1. Winter heating	40–45% of the average home owner's annual energy bill
2. Central air-conditioning	27%
3. Water heater	12% (higher with electric water heater)
4. Cooking	5% (higher with an electric range)
5. Refrigerator-freezer	4%
6. Clothes washer-dryer	3% (higher with electric dryer)
7. Small appliances & TV	2%
8. Other energy, including computers	2%

a factory house is not likely to fall down on any energy-conservation measures and is often leagues ahead of many codes. Depending on where you live, you could be taking chances with construction on a stickbuilt house. A manufactured house is, on the whole, more tightly built to prevent air leaks than its site-built cousin.

You would know this if you've ever worked outside on a bitter cold day. As skilled as a carpenter may be, it is difficult not to hurry a job on a frigid day in winter. Joints at the corners may show daylight; window framing, nailed up with a cold hammer held in an icy hand, could easily be looser than it should. Hastily putting insulation in, the carpenter may leave gaps. Other mistakes occur at other times, such as during those dog days in summer when workers are gasping for air and can easily slip up.

A house built under a roof in a factory is another story. Tight joints are par for the assembly line. And workers, under weather-protected conditions, can take the little extra time necessary to

Figure 12.1 *Traditional colonial house faces South today for maximum sunshine and heat entry in winter, just as the original settlers to New England designed it. The deep roof overhangs are authentic, too, for minimizing hot sun and heat entry in summer. Laubenstein house, manufactured by Adirondack Alternate Energy, Edinburgh, NY.*

see that things like insulation are snugly installed. A slipup is usually caught by the quality-control inspector before the house leaves the plant.

But even the insulation and other energy-saving specifications should be checked by a buyer, especially when the heating system and insulation are installed at the site. No matter what kind of house you buy, these are the important things to check.

■ Is There Enough Insulation? ■

Good insulation in the walls, floor and under the roof of a house is the Babe Ruth of energy-saving measures. It can cut winter heating bills by 30 to 35 percent, according to tests at the U.S. government's National Bureau of Standards.

Federal insulation standards apply to mobile homes, and state insulation codes apply to many factory houses with the exception of those shipped with no insulation in part or all of the house. This leaves the local builder or you to decide the amount of insulation to be installed.

Insulation, by the way, neither stops the loss of house heat in winter nor prevents heat coming into a house in summer. Nothing stops it. But insulation is the best solution to date for *slowing* the escape of heat from a sprint to a crawl; the more insulation, the more slowly the heat leaks out.

Insulation is measured by its R-value. This stands for "resistance to heat flow." A high R is good, a low one poor. The thicker the insulation, the higher the R-value; for example, 3 inches of fiberglass insulation has an R-value of about 12, depending on the brand; 6 inches an R of 20, more or less. The table that follows shows how much insulation to use according to the severity of the local climate measured by degree days.

The greater the number of degree days, the more cold weather in winter, thus the more insulation needed to keep heat from leaking out of a house. Annual degree days range from some 2,000 in the South for cities like Vicksburg, Mississippi, and Shreveport, Louisiana; about 5,000 in the colder North for cities like New York City, Pittsburgh and Kansas City; up to 9,000 or more in the coldest northern parts of such states as Maine and Minnesota. The degree days for your area can be obtained by a call to the nearest weather bureau station.

Insulation R-Values Recommended for a New House

Number of Degree Days	Ceilings	Walls	Floors over Unheated Space	Masonry Wall Insulation
0–3,000	R-19	R-12	R-11	R-3
3,000–5,000	R-30	R-14	R-19	R-11
5,000–6,650	R-30	R-18	R-19	R-11
6,650 or more	R-38	R-18	R-19	R-11

The insulation put in your house should meet at least the amount recommended in the table. This advice applies whether you buy a manufactured house that comes with insulation installed in the factory, or after delivery at your site.

■ WHAT KIND OF INSULATION? ■

Mineral wool insulation, which includes glass wool and fiberglass, is fine all-around insulation. It's a nonorganic material that's naturally bug-proof and fire-resistant. It's usually best to specify it rather than cellulose (a chopped-up newsprint product), which requires chemical treatment for fire-resistance and bug-proofing. Even when supposedly chemically treated, some cellulose brands are still not as good as they should be. Stick with mineral wool.

There are styrofoam and urethane insulations, the two most efficient kinds that could be used in houses. They are more costly than mineral wool but can pay for themselves when used for board insulation, such as wall sheathing or foundation board insulation.

■ INSULATING GLASS ■

That means double-pane and triple-pane window glass. It's made of parallel sheets of glass with a space between each sheet. Double-pane glass cuts the heat leakage, or loss, through windows by roughly 50 percent, compared with single-pane glass; triple-pane glass cuts the heat loss down to one-third that of single-pane glass.

In winter, the inside glass surface of multiglass windows is also less cold than the inside surface of single-pane. As a result, fewer cold downdrafts are created on the inside of insulating windows. In other words, insulating glass not only saves heat, but it also means a more comfortable house interior.

Double-glass windows are recommended for all houses in a climate with 3,000 degree days or more in winter; with electric

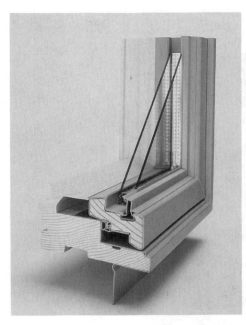

Figure 12.2 *Double-pane high-efficiency insulating glass can cut heat loss from a house in winter by up to 50 percent. In summer, it can reduce heat entry by 41 percent. Hence lower energy bills year round. Photo of Andersen ® High Performance™ insulating glass courtesy of Andersen Windows, Inc.*

heat it's recommended down to 2,000 degree days, according to studies by the National Bureau of Standards. Triple-glass windows will pay for themselves in fuel savings and comfort in a climate with 5,500 degree days or more.

Insulating glass, however, is generally not worthwhile in the South for a house with air conditioning only. That means not worthwhile in air-conditioned houses in a southern climate with fewer than 3,000 degree days in winter, or, in a house with electric heat, fewer than 2,000 degree days.

■ WEATHERSTRIPPING ■

Made of fiber, plastic or metal strips, weather stripping is installed around windows and doors to prevent air leaks in and out of a house. Such leaks are epidemic and are stopped only when weatherstripping is used to give a tight fit between a window and door and the stationary frame around each. Examine your present windows to see how weatherstripping is used to

Figure 12.3 *Many glass options for windows and doors feature high-performance heat mirror glass or low "E" glass. These high-efficiency glass options can help keep the home cooler in summer and warmer in winter. Photo of country kitchen courtesy of Greatwood Log & Cedar Homes, Elkhart Lake, Wisc.*

prevent air leaks; without weatherstripping, you'll see cracks and crevices of open light through which heat can leak out in winter. Every window and door for a house obviously should come with good weatherstripping.

■ CHOOSE THE LOWEST-COST ■ HEATING FUEL

Use gas heat when possible. Depending on where you live, electric heat costs from two to *four times* as much as heating with natural gas. So what homebuyer in his or her right mind would heat with electricity? Unfortunately, people buy houses without checking on the relative cost of different fuels—and then pay dearly.

Also, depending on where you live, oil heat can run from 50 percent to more than 100 percent more than heating with natural gas. It depends on where you live because gas prices, like electric rates, vary from one area to another. Fuel oil prices are relatively uniform throughout the country.

Natural gas has long been cheaper than oil and electricity for home heating. Unless the energy picture changes sharply, gas is still the cheapest choice for home heating and the best for lowest heating bills, and oil next.

■ COMPARING FUEL COSTS ■

Here's how to determine the lowest-price heating energy in your area. It depends on the comparative price of gas, oil and electricity. The table on the next page, developed by the Small Homes Council of the University of Illinois, is based on the unit price of each type of energy.

To use the table, determine the price charged for each fuel in your area. The price of gas, electricity and oil for home heating is obtainable by telephone calls to gas and electric companies and an oil dealer; LP (*liquid petroleum*) gas from an LP dealer. Ask for the local cost of gas and electricity for home heating and emphasize that you want the *actual* average unit price for home heating. Armed with the heating cost of each energy source, go to

How Fuels Compare in Cost			
Electricity (¢/kilowatt-hour)	*#2 Fuel Oil (¢/gal.)*	*Natural Gas (¢/therm)*	*LP (propane) Gas* (¢/gal.)*
0.5¢	14.3¢	10.2¢	9.9¢
1.0	28.7	20.5	18.9
1.5	43.0	30.7	28.4
2.0	57.4	41.0	37.7
2.5	71.7	51.2	47.3
3.0	86.1	61.5	56.6
4.0	114.8	82.0	75.4
5.0	143.5	102.5	94.3
6.0	172.2	123.0	113.1
8.5	215.2	153.7	141.4

*For LP butane gas, use the price of natural gas per therm from the table.
Source: The Small Homes Council, University of Illinois.

the table. It gives the equivalent prices for each heat horizontally across each line. For example, electricity at a cost of 3 cents a kilowatt-hour (kwh) for heating is equivalent to heating with oil at 86.1 cents a gallon and natural gas at 61.5 cents a therm.

If the cost of oil is less than 86.1 cents a gallon and natural gas is less than 61.5 cents a therm, heating with either will cost less than electricity at 3 cents per kwh. If oil costs you, say, 80 cents a gallon, it will cost less than heating with 3 cents electricity. If natural gas costs you 40 cents a therm locally, it costs roughly one-third the bill for heating with 3 cents electricity and 86 cents oil.

Which energy is cheapest of all for heating your house? The table tells you.

The price of oil is also as volatile as the shifting politics in the Mideast where much of our oil comes from. You can never tell when its price may rise or fall, which doesn't make for peace of mind.

■ OTHER FUEL FACTS ■

Consider a few other things when choosing among gas, oil and electricity. Electric heat is the cheapest and easiest to install in a house. That's why it may be put in new houses even though it costs more to operate. Gas is the next lowest in installation cost and oil the most expensive, especially because it requires an oil tank, too.

The actual operating bills with electric heat can be less than estimated because it's easy to install a separate thermostat in each room. The heat in any room can be easily turned off to save money, whereas this is more difficult to do with gas or oil heat. In addition, electric heating usually requires less service and maintenance than oil or gas heat.

Moral: If the local cost of electricity is not *much* more expensive than gas or oil heat, electric heat can make sense. In other words, if electric heat will cost up to 20 percent more than gas or oil, according to the preceding table, its other economies can offset its apparent higher operating cost. But be sure that electric heat meets this guideline. Once it's installed, it's expensive to switch to other heat.

Less is at stake when choosing between oil and gas fuel. If you find out that you chose a loser and the other fuel will cost less, it's usually easy to switch from oil to gas, or vice versa, with a minimum of expense. Only the burner mechanism usually has to be replaced. The rest of the heating unit remains the same. Check that the furnace or boiler you get with your house can operate with either a gas or an oil burner.

■ COAL AND WOOD HEATING ■

Can you save with coal or wood? A lot of people give each serious attention. Together, they represent only about 1 percent of the home fuel market, but this can change. For the first time in years, coal sales by retail dealers to homes, churches, small commercial establishments and so on, between January 1977 and January 1978 rose by 1 million tons. An indication of the demand for wood comes from Long Island, New York. In 1973, firewood sold there for about $45 a cord. Five years later, in December 1978, the increased demand had pushed the price up so much that people were lucky to find a cord for under $125. The price later fell to $100 or less.

Where coal is available for home use, it is likely to be less expensive than other fuels, according to the National Coal Association. An association spokesperson said that greater numbers of people probably would not be attracted to coal heating. You usually must buy a coal furnace, and once in use continually cleaning it out and discarding the ashes is no pleasant chore. He acknowledges that a small but growing number of people are buying and using small wood/coal stoves in living spaces to supplement, and in some cases replace, conventional central heat. The burning of coal, however, is an environmental concern, which discourages its use.

If you can pick up wood free, it's a distinct advantage. But if you buy it, the cost could be as high as that for gas or oil fuel. Take into account the amount of wood required for house heat and the energy content of wood.

In general, one cord of firewood at $100 a cord is equivalent to:

Electric Heat	#2 Fuel Oil	Natural Gas	LP Gas
at 3¢/kwh	at 80¢/gal	at 60¢/therm	at 55¢/gal

These comparisons use a wood stove efficiency of 50 percent. Based on these figures, if your electric rate is 4 cents per kwh, wood at $100 a cord may turn out to be cheaper. But natural gas at, say, 35 cents a therm or oil at 45 cents a gallon would be nearly half the cost of $100 wood.

■ FIVE OTHER WAYS TO KEEP DOWN ■
HEATING BILLS

Here are fundamental tips that you may have heard before. They're worth repeating even though you need not worry when you buy a new, up-to-date manufactured house outfitted with good, modern appliances and equipment. They do apply if you buy a used factory-made house.

Get the proper-size heating unit. Heating units are measured by their Btu output (e.g., 86,000 Btu per hour), and bigger is not better. A Btu stands for British thermal unit, the standard measure of heat quantity. One Btu is equal to the amount of heat required to raise the temperature of a pound of water by one degree F. A heating unit—warm air furnace or hot water heating boiler—with an output greater than your house requirements will burn more fuel than necessary.

Use a new high-efficiency heating unit. New gas and oil house heaters can cut home heating costs by 50 percent, compared with conventional heaters. These units will save you a lot of money, particularly if you live in a northern climate. Although high-efficiency heating units should be in nearly all new factory houses, you can't be sure unless you check before buying.

Get a vent damper. With gas or oil heat, it can cut your heating bill as much as 20 percent. A damper is installed in the flue pipe that carries the exhaust gases from the heating unit to the chimney. It closes when the heating unit goes off and thereby prevents residual heat from escaping up the chimney, and it also prevents cold air from coming down the chimney and chilling the heating unit.

A fail-safe device is included with an electronically operated damper. When the house thermostat calls for heat, it first signals the damper to open. If the damper refuses to open, the burner will not light. This prevents the possibility of flue gases dissipating into the house. Most heating unit makers offer vent dampers with their equipment. You can save money by specifying one with your heating unit.

Install an electronic spark ignition. This eliminates a continuously burning pilot on gas furnaces. A thermostat-controlled spark ignites the pilot, which lights the burner. When heat is not needed, the gas is turned off. Most modern heaters should have this device.

Specify an automatic-clock heating thermostat. It can cut fuel bills 7 to 15 percent, depending on your climate. It automatically tells the heating system to doze off and provide less heat (*setback*) to the house at night when you sleep. It's also set to turn up the house heat at whatever time you want more heat when you awake. It will pay for itself in savings. One kind provides a double setback: one at night; the other for daytime when all members of a family are regularly away from home. Each degree of setback in winter, day or night, will save approximately 3 percent of the energy used at the higher setting. The same 3 percent saving applies in summer with a cooling system.

Be sure that vulnerable heating and cooling ducts are insulated, which means exposed ducts in unheated and non-air-conditioned parts of your house, e.g., a crawl space under the house; a hot attic above.

Get a high-efficiency water heater. Because the water heater that provides hot water to the kitchen, bathroom and laundry is a big energy guzzler, a good one can obviously save more than a few bucks on monthly energy bills. Here are pointers for getting a good self-contained water heater and storage tank, the most common kind.

Specify a water heater operated by natural gas, unless gas is unavailable. Like central heating, a gas water heater is lower in cost to use than an oil or electric heater. Even in a house with electric central heat, a gas water heater usually is more economical than an electric one.

Get a high-efficiency water heater, which means a super-insulated tank. It costs a little more than standard models, but its high efficiency will repay that extra price in annual operating savings.

■ APPLIANCES ■

Cook with gas. Electric cooking can be decidedly more expensive.

Gas range and oven. It should have instant ignition. Also, a self-cleaning oven may not save energy, but it saves nasty work and you can give yourself a break.

A microwave oven, while not for all-around cooking, saves energy for what it cooks. In baking four potatoes, for example, it uses 61 percent less energy than a standard electric oven requires.

Refrigerator. High-efficiency refrigerators with improved insulation are practically standard now. They save 10 percent over older models.

Dishwasher. Be sure to get a dishwasher with a control that eliminates the drying cycle.

Clothes dryer. Get one with a "drying sensor." This gauge tells when the clothes are dry. If all moisture is gone before the drying cycle ends, the sensor turns off the machine.

Clothes washer. Researchers have found that 80° F water will clean clothes as well as 120° F water—the difference between "warm" and "hot" settings on machines.

■ CENTRAL AIR CONDITIONING ■

Specify a high-efficiency air conditioner. That means one with an *energy efficiency ratio* (EER) of 7.5 or better, and preferably 10. Practically speaking, avoid the cheapest kind for room or house. The little extra cost for high quality pays off, including quiet operation as well as high efficiency.

Be sure that the cooling unit is sized properly for your house.

Like house heating, an oversized cooling unit is an energy waster. In addition, too big a cooler fails to perform an important summer job: dehumidifying the air. This advice also applies to room units.

■ WHAT ABOUT THE FIREPLACE? ■

Unfortunately, many a new fireplace installed up to a few years ago lost heat up the chimney. You can minimize such waste largely by following the fireplace instructions that come with the house. Excellent new prefab fireplaces are now available in manufactured houses. It's up to you, though, to be sure that you get an efficient, up-to-date model. Check in advance that the fireplace has these features:

1. A damper with a positive close.
2. A glass fire screen (alas) to prevent loss of furnace-delivered heat. It gives total assurance against the danger of fire from flying embers, but still provides the radiant heat given off by the fire.
3. Air-circulating vents. At a little extra cost, these are fireplace forms with air-flow ducts that capture more of the fire's heat. They deliver it safely to the room served by the fireplace, and, in some cases, to adjoining rooms.

How To Use Free Solar Heat and Cut Home Energy Bills

A couple I'll call the Jacksons made their bed right when they bought their factory house not long ago. They made sure that the house would face south on their land and trap big loads of solar heat in winter. As a result, their fuel bills run sharply lower than those of friends who live in a similar house across the street. In summer some of the same measures that cut heating bills in winter also help make their house easier to cool and hence lower air-conditioning bills.

Big fuel savings have been documented in manufactured houses that are specially designed for what's called *passive* solar heat. That awkward phrase, apparently coined by an engineer, means opening up a house properly to take full advantage of all the solar heat that's free without an expensive mechanical solar heating system. In other words, without a roof collector, pipes, valves, etc., which is called *active* solar heating.

Independent engineers did a study of one house, for example, made by Green Mountain Homes of Royalton, Vermont, designed for maximum solar heat efficiency. The study showed that during a bitter Vermont winter the house was heated for eight months for only $249. Free solar heat helped to cut the heating bill by more than 50 percent.

In addition to facing a house south, two other requirements are necessary to trap solar heat in a house: plenty of window glass facing the south sun and the means to circulate the solar heat inside.

About the only other way to achieve the same end is to build your house on a turntable that can be revolved at will, turning it around to the southern sun in winter and turning it around 180 degrees in the summer so it faces the cool north.

If you can't swing a turntable, you can profit considerably by properly orienting your house. The annual energy savings that result not only run as high as 50 percent, compared with a random exposure and design; your house also will be brighter and more cheerful in more than one way, for example, potentially higher resale value.

■   THE IDEAL EXPOSURE   ■

The ideal exposure for most houses in the northern hemisphere is broadside to the south, because in winter the sun rises in the southeast and sets in the southwest, as shown in the diagram. In summer, the sun rises in the northeast, travels a higher arc across the sky, being almost directly overhead at noon, and sets in the northwest. Scientific facts emphasize what this means:

1. Only rooms with windows that face from southeast to southwest receive much sunshine and solar heat in the dead of winter. In case the importance of that escapes anyone, window glass can let an enormous amount of sun heat pour into a house. It's the greenhouse effect, the phenomenon that makes a greenhouse hot.
2. Every room on the south side of a house receives five times as much sun heat in winter as in summer.
3. East and west rooms, on the other hand, receive six times as much sun heat in summer as in winter.
4. Rooms and windows facing north receive virtually no sunshine at all in winter and some in summer; the farther

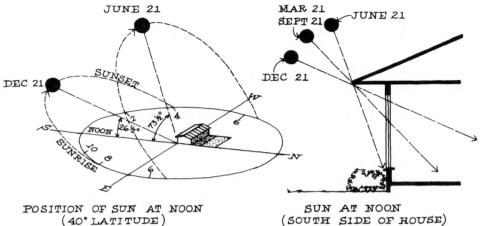

POSITION OF SUN AT NOON
(40° LATITUDE)

SUN AT NOON
(SOUTH SIDE OF HOUSE)

Figure 13.1 *A house or its main windows clearly must face south or close to it to trap any real quantity of solar heat in winter. This diagram applies to all houses in the northern hemisphere; it's the reverse in the southern hemisphere. But in summer the same south-facing windows can be easily shaded from hot overhead sun with roof overhangs, since the sun comes in from a higher overhead angle. Shading can also be provided, of course, by trees or awnings. Source: © A.M. Watkins.*

south you are, the more sunshine is shed on the north side in summer.

Clearly, a house with a lot of glass facing south can let enough heat pour in that your furnace can rest for much of the day—hence major fuel savings. That's accomplished without mechanical solar collector panels on the roof, expensive pipes and ducts or other means of distributing solar heat the mechanical way.

Unfortunately, housing experts have concluded that mechanical solar heating systems for houses are still far from practical. They are not working any better, alas, than our efforts to extract pure water from our oceans. Solar water heaters for houses were the only solar units with promise in houses, and these can pay off only as an alternative to high-cost electric water heaters. That means it pays off only if you cannot use a gas or oil water heater, both of which should be considerably cheaper to operate. In short, mechanical solar heating systems are unproven in houses.

■ HOW TO USE FREE SOLAR HEAT ■
IN YOUR HOUSE

This is a wholly different ballgame and it's eminently practical—
and cheap.

1. *Try first for a site on which your house can be given a good southern exposure.* The ideal lot is one on the south side of the street. Land on any side of the street often can work well if it offers flexibility. It will also help, of course, if you have a good view toward the south. Remember that it's perfectly all right for the back of a house to face the street. It helps, too, if the back is not unattractive.

2. *Choose a house that can easily face south, the Mecca direction for solar heat.* It doesn't have to be due south. Tests show that excellent solar heating can result when a house faces up to about 30 degrees east or west of due south. If necessary, have windows added on the long south side, while eliminating as many as possible from other sides of the house. Most home manufacturers will gladly make window changes in their houses.

   Actually, the house itself can face any direction. The important thing to remember is to have the windows of your daytime living areas (kitchen, dining and family rooms) facing south for sunlight to flood in. A southern exposure is less important for the living room, unless you use it often during the day.

   Bedrooms obviously need less daytime sun and best face the north or east. On the east, you may welcome the bright sun and free heat flooding in first thing in the morning. Bedrooms on the west can get furnace-hot in summer by the time you are ready for bed. Try to locate the garage or carport on the west as a sun shield in summer, or on the north as a wind shield in winter.

   Little or no window glass should be on the vulnerable, windlashed north side of your house to keep winter heat losses from the house down to a minimum. That includes a wall exposure ranging from northeast around to west, depending on the prevailing wind in winter.

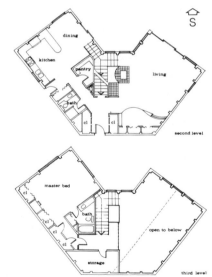

Figure 13.2 *This house is virtually loaded with glass on its south side to let in great amounts of sunshine and warming heat in winter. Result is rockbottom fuel bills in the frigid winter cold of northern New York. The structure, of course, is well insulated, and all windows are made with insulating glass. Smith house. From* House Warming *by Susan Aulisi and Doug McGilvary. © 1983. Published by Adirondack Alternate Energy, Edinburgh, NY.*

You can get good weather protection in winter with a windbreak of evergreen trees on the north, as is frequently seen near farmhouses in the wind-scourged Great Plains. If you live in the South, a south orientation may be less desirable. You will have more shade if a house faces north, with the patio on the north or northeast.

3. *Have good summer sun control built into the house.* The beauty of facing windows to the sunny south is that south windows are comparatively easy to shade from hot summer sun. Hot sun blasting down on window glass in summer is, in fact, the second largest cause of high air-conditioning bills. (The first is hot sun on the roof all day long.) Shading windows from direct sun can mean not only sharply reduced air-conditioning bills in summer but also a cooler house without air-conditioning.

Roof overhangs are one of the best ways to shade southern windows from direct sun in summer. A roof overhang can easily keep out the summer sun. But in winter, the sun sails under the overhangs and into the house through the same windows because the sun is shining in from a much lower angle in the sky. The farther north a house is located, the deeper the overhang necessary to keep out the summer sun. The manufacturer of the house you buy can tell you how deep that southern roof overhangs must be for good sun shading in your latitude.

4. *Keep the sun heat inside after you've caught it.* First of all, this calls for a house that is very well insulated and, except in the warm South, has double- or triple-glass windows. Solar heat from the sun can pour in through multipane glass virtually as easily as through ordinary single-pane glass, so double or triple glass is fine for trapping solar heat. But heat inside a house has a different wave length. It can leak out quite easily through single-pane glass, the thinnest and least energy-conserving kind of glass, but not so easily through multipane glass. Multipane glass windows generally do not pay in the warm South for either heating or central air conditioning, as noted previously.

5. *All other things being relatively equal, use forced warm air heat.* That means, of course, central heating with a fan that circulates the warm air heat around the house. The same blower and ducts are used to spread solar heat around the house. When no heat from the furnace is needed, the fan can be turned on to circulate solar heat in the south side of the house to the rest of the house.

6. *Store excess solar heat coming in during the day for use at night though, unfortunately, this is easier said than done.* Heat-absorbing materials inside the house are used to soak up sun heat in the house. When the sun sets, the same materials will release their heat to help keep the house warm. Such materials include brick, stone or concrete floor on the sun side of the house, or drums of water (though these are not the most attractive things to have in a house).

   The catch is that such heat-storage ideas have not been sufficiently developed and tested for use in houses. A solid concrete floor can work well in the houses with passive solar heat mentioned earlier in this chapter, but one sparrow doesn't make a summer.

   To find out, ask house manufacturers and their salespeople when you shop for a house. What are good things to build into a house to trap, store and circulate solar heat? How can you use them in your house?

Don't take no for an answer when you request a house that can make natural use of solar heat. It's been around for a long time. Smart builders and architects have been using it in houses throughout the world for hundreds of years.

Tips on Buying Manufactured Houses

Here are a few tips and a review of the facts about manufactured houses that deserve special mention.

■ CHOOSE THE RIGHT LAND OR SITE ■

Choosing the right land or site is obviously the key to making it easy for a house to face south and be easy and cheap to heat and cool, particularly if you buy a factory house in a development or a mobile home in a mobile home park. A worldwide energy crisis caused a major reappraisal of house design in the United States. The orientation of a house in relation to the sun and cold winter winds is important.

A house doesn't have to face due south but can face up to 30 degrees or so east or west of due south. Best of all is a lot on the south side of the street with the house and its big windows facing the rear of the lot.

If you buy a private lot of your own, its geographical location obviously can make a big difference in your living and in the future resale value of your house. In addition to putting a high priority on a southern exposure, here are other matters to check:

- The local zoning should ensure that the area maintains its residential character. No one wants a gas station across the street.

- There also should be good local transportation, good schools if you have children, convenient nearby shopping, churches, parks or other recreational facilities and no nuisance neighbors, such as an airport, noisy highway or disco bar next door.

- The cost of improving the land can be greatly reduced if the utilities (gas, water, electricity and sewage disposal) are readily available. Can each be obtained at minimum expense?

- What about water runoff and drainage from the land?

- Land improvement cost can be reduced if your house can be put down near the front of the lot. Then the utility lines from the street to the house (which you pay for) are shorter. You will also save on the cost of a driveway and walks.

■ USE A GOOD LOCAL BUILDER ■

Even the best factory house package can easily be sabotaged if assembled at your site by a hack builder (who can seem sincere and dependable when you first meet him or her).

One couple, for instance, hired a local builder recommended by a relative to erect a factory house. He had offered to do the job at a lower price than builders from the manufacturer's list of recommended builders.

Completion of the house was botched, and the couple complained to the manufacturer. The manufacturer pointed out examples of sheer carelessness, including mistakes showing that the builder hadn't bothered to read the assembly instructions. "Obviously, we are not responsible," the factory representative told them. "Read your contract," he said.

The couple could not get the guilty builder to make amends; in fact, he couldn't be found. Moral: Read your contract carefully, and also be sure that the local builder who puts your house package together is really good, even if you must pay a competent professional a higher price than a low-bid builder with unproved ability. That extra price is, in effect, an insurance premium paid for your protection.

■ BUILDING YOUR OWN HOUSE ■

Don't bite off more than you can chew. Building a house from a factory package, or kit, can put you leagues ahead of the game, compared with building a stickbuilt house starting from scratch, as mentioned earlier. But it's still not child's play, even for a skilled do-it-yourself person. Putting up a whole house is the do-it-yourself equivalent of climbing the Matterhorn, the supreme peak.

As noted earlier, building your own house from a kit generally requires six months to a year. The completion time depends on how much is done by special skilled labor, as well as the time you can give to the work. Some people choose to do most of the construction themselves. Others choose to have such difficult work as the foundation, basic structure and the wiring, plumbing and heating provided by specialists. Even if you subcontract major portions of the construction, you can still save considerably by building your own house. That's because labor by itself accounts for—brace yourself—only about 16 percent of the sales price of a new house, according to the NAHB and the U.S. Department of Commerce.

Almost twice that money goes for building materials (30 percent). The rest goes for land (24 percent), the cost of financing construction of the house (14 percent), builder's operating costs (12 percent) and profit (4 percent). Significant savings can be made on the land, by being your own contractor.

■ GETTING A HIGH-QUALITY FACTORY HOUSE ■

In Chapter 8, I mentioned why a mobile home and all other houses can pass tough building codes but still lack uniformly high-quality construction. A building code applies *only* to those parts of a house that affect the health and safety of people. The quality of much of the rest of a house can be borderline, if not low, and your health and safety will not be in jeopardy.

The water heater, for example, may be absolutely safe in operation but not very energy-efficient, and thus you may have high energy bills. You may have to work overtime to keep kitchen and bathroom floors looking good because of low-quality flooring. Other parts of the house can quickly become frayed and unattractive, but that's par for the course.

A truly efficient water heater, good flooring and other such products will mean low upkeep and long life, but they are not covered by building codes. They tend to be the parts of a house that a home manufacturer, like a local home builder, is not likely to spend more money on than necessary for high quality. A good part of the reason is that homebuyers generally will not pay extra for a house of uniformly high-quality construction. Most buyers will go down the street, or to another home manufacturer, to buy a cheaper house. In self-defense, therefore, manufacturers say they are compelled to concentrate on using the lowest-cost parts and products to keep down their house price tags. Naturally, that's no formula for good quality, which costs more.

The extra cost of high-quality materials is often less than many people think. Paying extra for really good-quality products and materials where it can count, as noted below, can increase the cost of a typical house by a mere 5 to 8 percent, according to a study by *House & Home* magazine. That will mean a relatively small increase in your down payment and monthly mortgage payments, but this will be offset many times over in reduced upkeep and house operating costs. A good example is getting a permanent-finish outside wall surface. This can save the cost of repainting, or a periodic expenditure of up to several thousand dollars.

You be the judge. If you expect to stay in your house less than five years, paying extra for a better house may be a questionable investment, except that it can make the house sell for you at a higher price. If you expect to own it more than five years, the longer you're in the house, the more a high-quality house

makes good financial sense. You'll get your money back com-
pounded, not only in savings in upkeep and service, but also
in pleasure.

Here are the most likely places to check for quality and, if
necessary, to spend a little more money for better-than-ordinary
quality products furnished with any house or mobile home you
buy. This doesn't mean, by the way, that you must pay high
prices for top-of-the-line quality. Many products are made in
three or four steps up in quality, and merely stepping up to the
second level above dead bottom can make a big difference—and
at comparatively small extra cost.

- *Kitchen fixtures, appliances, cabinets and flooring.* The extra price
  for a high-efficiency refrigerator and a good dishwasher will
  pay for itself in monthly operating savings and reduced
  service, no question about it. Good fixtures, good cabinets
  and good flooring will reduce cleaning and upkeep as well as
  prolong attractiveness.

- *The bathroom.* Get a good sink (lavatory), tub and toilet, which
  means adequate size as well as solid design and construction,
  as described in detail in Chapter 11.

- *Furnace and water heater.* A high-efficiency furnace and
  water heater should be top priority requirements. Without them, you're a sitting duck for higher-than-necessary
  energy bills.

- *Exterior walls.* An outside wall, like long-life brick, stone or
  vinyl and aluminum siding, can save a small fortune over the
  years in repainting costs.

- *Windows and doors.* Getting good quality here includes
  specifying double- or triple-pane window glass than a
  glass facing north (in the Northern Hemisphere), and tight-
  fitting windows and doors, i.e., with good weatherstripping
  all over.

■   FINANCING A MANUFACTURED HOUSE   ■

As with buying a stickbuilt house, this means getting a mortgage loan with a down payment and monthly repayments that you can live with and no small-print hooks. The importance of shopping for one cannot be overemphasized. Yet some people will spend more time shopping for steak and potatoes than for the home loan document that can tie them up for tens of thousands of dollars for years and years.

Sometimes, of course, just finding a bank or other lender who will give you a mortgage can be difficult, and like a beggar, you must take what's given. But at other times, lenders have money for mortgages coming out of their ears, and mortgage shopping can be the equivalent of gunning down targets in a shooting gallery: You can take your pick. It depends on the state of the national market for mortgage money; sometimes plenty of money is available for mortgages, other times not.

In any case, call banks, savings and loan associations, mortgage brokers and anyone else a manufacturer may recommend for a mortgage loan on these houses. Find out from each lender the mortgage interest rate, down payment and number of years to repay. In addition, ask about such small-print provisions as a prepayment penalty fee if you repay any portion of the mortgage ahead of when it's due. That includes paying it off if you sell the house before the mortgage has been repaid. It's best when there's no prepayment penalty after a year or two from the date you get the mortgage.

Does the mortgage lender have the right to raise the interest rate? The lender should not, with one exception—with an adjustable rate mortgage, the interest rate can go down as well as up according to national interest rates for all money. Do you have to pay *points* for a mortgage? That's a special charge that can amount to hundreds, if not thousands, of dollars. And very important, what will the total *closing costs* bill be? That's for the fees and special charges related to obtaining a mortgage; e.g., title insurance, mortgage "commitment" fee, and so on.

But also remember that often the terms of a mortgage loan and its closing costs are negotiable, particularly when a banker's ears are brimful of money. In other words, you can bargain for better terms than offered. Do you want a lower interest rate? Smaller down payment and cheaper closing costs? Ask for them. Don't be shy. After all, *your* money is at stake. Merely speaking up for the best deal can earn respect, assuming that you handle the request in a calm, businesslike way.

▲ PART 2 ▲
Finding the Right Manufacturer for Your House

A Directory of Home Manufacturers

Here are the names, addresses and phone numbers of more than 260 manufacturers of factory-made houses in the United States and Canada. To find out if a manufacturer offers a toll-free 800 number, call 800-555-1212. Listed below are the types of homes available from U.S. and Canadian manufacturers.

U.S. Manufacturers

- Dome houses

- Modular houses

- Panelized houses

- Precut houses

- Log homes

Canadian Manufacturers

- Modular homes

- Panelized and preengineered houses

- Log homes (handcrafted, profiled and timberframe)

Many manufacturers will ship houses at least 200 to 300 miles away from their plant. Some will ship considerably farther, including across the country. However, shipping charges can run as much as a thousand dollars or more. You may find that the house is still worth it. At least one couple agrees. They live in California and paid cross-country shipping charges to buy a manufactured house made in New England. Some manufacturers have distribution centers in various parts of the country, though their main plant is in Massachusetts. One important point to note: You do not pay for it until it has been delivered.

New England is the home of many manufacturers of notably well-designed houses. Pennsylvania has the largest number of modular home manufacturers (many ship long distances as far away as northern New England). North Carolina has the greatest number of log home makers. In addition, many home manufacturers are concentrated in the Pacific Northwest. No matter where you live in the United States, it is very likely that there are several home manufacturers of one type or another who will be delighted to sell you a house and deliver it to you.

The major trade association in manufactured houses is the Building Systems Council of the National Association of Home Builders (15th & M Streets NW, Washington, DC 20005; 202-822-0576). The mobile homes trade association is the Manufactured Housing Institute (1745 Jefferson Davis Highway, Suite 511, Arlington, VA 22202; 703-413-6620). Call or write to them for their booklet on "How To Buy a Mobile Home."

The major trade association for manufactured houses in Canada is the Canadian Manufactured Housing Association (CMHA, 150 Laurier Ave. West, Ottawa, Ontario, Canada K1P 5J4; 613-563-3520). The mobile homes trade association is the Canadian Manufactured Housing Institute (CMHI), which you can reach at the same address and phone number.

■ U.S. HOME MANUFACTURERS ■

Dome Houses

A dome is the quintessential structure. Not only is it superstrong it also encloses a maximum of living space with a minimum of surface, hence reducing construction materials and labor, and energy bills as much as 40 percent than for a conventional house (largely because of one-third less exposed surface).

Compared to other manufactured houses, a dome can be comparatively simple to build, providing that you thoroughly investigate dome houses before you buy. What materials are provided? How well do the parts go together? Look for clear and simple instructions, especially if you plan to build it yourself.

As for all factory houses, the foundation must be accurately built according to specifications. Another important consideration is obtaining a leakproof roof. This generally requires conventional roof shingles, such as asphalt or wood, installed according to the standards used for conventional houses.

The number of dome house manufacturers is growing, so be sure to deal with a reputable, established company.

The dome makers listed here with an asterisk are members of the National Dome Committee of the Building Systems Council.

American Geodesics, Inc.
1505 Webster St.
Richmond, VA 23220
804-643-3184

American Ingenuity Inc.*
3500 Harlock Rd.
Melbourne, FL 32934
407-254-4220

Domes America, Inc.*
6345 W. Joliet Rd.
Countryside, IL 60525
708-579-9400

Geodesic Domes and Homes*
607 Hwy. 110 North
P.O. Box 575
Whitehouse, TX 75791
903-839-2000

Geodesic Domes, Inc.*
10290 Davison Rd.
Davison, MI 48423
313-653-2383

Helikon Design Corporation
P.O. Box 48
Cavetown, MD 21720
301-824-2254

Natural Spaces Domes
37955 Bridge Rd.
North Branch, MN 55056
800-733-7107

American Geodesics
1505 Webster St.
Richmond, VA 23220
804-643-3184

Oregon Dome, Inc.*
3215 Meadow Lane
Eugene, OR 97402
503-689-3443

Timberline Geodesic Inc.*
2015 Blake St.
Berkeley, CA 94704
415-849-4881

**Semispheres Building
Systems, Inc.,** division of

Modular Houses (also called Sectional Houses)

Modular houses are 95 percent or more complete when they are shipped from the factory. They're generally shipped in two or more sections, 12 or 14 feet wide, one story high and up to 60 feet long. Two or more sections may be combined at the site to make a complete house, apartment or office building. Virtually all you need to do before moving in is connect it to outside sources for energy, water and sewer.

Members of the Modular Building Systems Council

The following home manufacturers are members of the Modular Building Systems Council, one of four separate national building councils under the aegis of the Building Systems Councils of the National Association of Home Builders (NAHB). The other three councils are for home manufacturers of panelized, dome and log homes.

Home manufacturer members of the councils "pledge to adhere to the Building Systems Business Creed—which assures consumers of high quality materials and standards of workmanship, along with fair, frank and honest business practices." In addition to affiliation with the NAHB, members of the Building Systems Councils are members of a state or local Home Builders Association.

Active Homes Corporation
7938 South Van Dyke
Marlette, MI 48453
517-635-3532

All American Homes, Inc.
1418 S. 13th St.
Decatur, IN 46733
219-724-9171

Alouette Homes
P.O. Box 187
Newport, VT 05855
514-539-3100

Beaver Mountain Log Homes
RD 1, Box 32
Hancock, NY 13783
607-467-2700

Bradbury Corporation
111 Frontage Rd South
Pacific, WA 98047
206-833-3113

Cardinal Homes, Inc.
P.O. Box 10, Highway 15
Wylliesburg, VA 23976
804-735-8111

Chelsea Homes, Inc.
Rt. 9W, P.O. Box 599
Marlboro, NY 12542
914-236-3311

The Conifer Group
3140 S.E. Hawthorne Blvd.
Portland, OR 97214
503-239-0015

Contempri Industries, Inc.
P.O. Box 69
1000 W. Water St.
Pinckneyville, IL 62274
618-357-5361

Customized Structures, Inc.
P.O. Box 884, Plains Road
Claremont, NH 03743
603-543-1236

Deluxe Homes of PA, Inc.
499 W. Third St.
P.O. Box 323
Berwick, PA 18603
717-752-5914

Design Homes, Inc.
P.O. Box 411
West 5th St.
Mifflinville, PA 18631
717-752-1001

DKM Building Enterprises
P.O. Box 246, Rte. 442E
Muncy, PA 17756
717-546-2261

Dynamic Homes Inc.
525 Roosevelt Ave.
Detroit Lakes, MN 56501
218-847-2611

Epoch Corporation
P.O. Box 235
Pembroke, NH 03275
603-225-3907

Excel Homes, Inc.
RD 2, Box 683
Liverpool, PA 17045
717-444-3395

**The Future Homes
Technology Inc.**
P.O. Box 4255
33 Ralph Street
Port Jervis, NY 12771
914-856-9033

General Housing Corp.
900 Andre St.
Bay City, MI 48706
517-684-8078

Glen River Industries
1703 Lum Rd.
Centralia, WA 98531
206-736-1341

Haven Homes, Inc.
P.O. Box 178, Route 150
Beech Creek, PA 16822
717-962-2111

Heckaman Homes
P.O. Box 229
26331 U.S. #6 East
Nappanee, IN 46550
219-773-4167

Homes of Merit
P.O. Box 1606
Bartow, FL 33830
813-533-0593

Huntington Homes, Inc.
P.O. Box 98, Route 14
East Montpelier, VT 05651
802-479-3625

Integri Homes
P.O. Box 491655
Leesburg, FL 34749
904-787-2056

Kan-Build, Inc.
Heartland Homes
Nichols Rd. and Hwy 31
P.O. Box 259
Osage City, KS 66523
913-528-4163

Kaplan Building Systems, Inc.
Route 433 East, P.O. Box 247
Pine Grove, PA 17963
717-345-4635

Miller Residential
P.O. Box 1283
28384 CR #20 West
Elkhart, IN 46515
219-522-3002

Mod-U-Kraf Homes, Inc.
P.O. Box 573
Rocky Mount, VA 24151
703-483-0291

Nanticoke Homes, Inc.
P.O. Box F, U.S. Route 13
Greenwood, DE 19950
302-349-4561

Nationwide Homes, Inc.
P.O. Box 5511
1100 Rives Rd.
Martinsville, VA 24115
703-632-7101

**New Century Homes
Signature Building Systems**
P.O. Box 9
1100 W. Lake St.
Topeka, IN 46571
219-593-2962

New England Homes, Inc.
270 Ocean Rd.
Greenland, NH 03840
603-436-8830

North American Housing Corp.
4011 Rock Hall Road
P.O. Box 145
Point of Rocks, MD 21777
301-694-9100

Northwest Pacific Manufacturing
2155 NE 238th Dr.
Troutdale, OR 97060
503-666-7128

Penn Lyon Homes, Inc.
101 Airport Road
P.O. Box 27
Selinsgrove, PA 17870
717-374-4004

Pre Built Structures, Inc.
N. 5315 Corrigan Road
Otis Orchards, WA 99027
509-928-1442

Princeton Homes Corporation
P.O. Box 2086
412 Princeton Road
Danville, VA 24541
804-797-3144

Randal Homes Corp.
129 North West St.
P.O. Box 337
Piketon, OH 45661
614-289-4770

Regional Building Systems Inc.
5560 Sterrett Place
Suite 200
Columbia, MD 21044
410-997-7200

Ritz-Craft Corporation of PA
P.O. Box 70
15 Industrial Park Road
Mifflinburg, PA 17844
717-966-1053

Rotec Industries
333 West Lake Street
Elmhurst, IL 60126
708-279-3300

Schult Homes Corporation
P.O. Box 219
Elkton, MD 21921
410-398-2100

The Scotsman Group, Inc.
8211 Town Center Dr.
Baltimore, MD 21236

Stratford Homes Ltd. Partnership
P.O. Box 37
Stratford, WI 54484
715-687-3133

Taylor Homes
Highway 71 North
P.O. Box 438
Anderson, MO 64831
417-845-3311

Terrace Homes
301 S. Main
P.O. Box 1040
Adams, WI 53910
608-339-7888

Unibilt Industries, Inc.
4671 Poplar Creek Road
P.O. Box 373
Vandalia, OH 45377
513-890-7570

Wausau Homes, Inc.
P.O. Box 8005

Wausau, WI 54402
715-359-7272

Westchester Modular Homes
30 Reagans Mill Rd.
Wingdale, NY 12594
914-832-9400

Other Modular Home Manufacturers

American Dream Modular Homes
P.O. Box 51116
Springfield, MA 01150
413-543-4590

AvisAmerica
Henry St.
Avis, PA 17721
800-AvisAmerica

Benchmark Industries
630 Hay Avenue
Brookville, OH 45309
513-833-4091

Clayton Homes
623 Market St.
Knoxville, TN 37901
615-970-7200

Customized Structures, Inc.*
P.O. Box 884, Plains Rd.
Claremont, NH 03743
603-543-1236

Golden West Homes
1801 E. Edinger #240
Santa Anna, CA 92705
714-835-4200

Hi-Tech Housing Inc.
19319 County Rd. 8
Bristol, IN 46507
219-848-5593

International Building Systems
5560 Sterrett Place
Suite 200
Columbia, MD 21044
410-997-7200

International Housing Division
999 S. Main St.
Smithfield, UT 84335
801-563-3232

Muncy Building Enterprises
P.O. Box 246, Rt. 442E
Muncy, PA 17756
717-546-2261

Poloron Products, Inc.
74 Ridge Rd., Box 187
Middleburg, PA 17840
717-837-5479

NVR, Inc.
100 Ryan Court
Pittsburgh, PA 15205
412-276-8000

Timberland Homes
1201 37th N.W.
Auburn, WA 98001
206-735-3435

Panelized Houses

Panelized describes the way a house is made in a factory and shipped (see Chapter 5). The walls and sometimes the floor and roof are made in panels, generally 8 feet high and from 4 to 40 feet long. The panels can be quickly lined up and connected at the site, and the house shell, erected and closed in one to three weeks.

Members of the Panelized Building Systems Council

Acorn Structures
P.O. Box 1445
Concord, MA 01742
508-369-4111

Beaver Mountain Log Homes
RD 1, Box 32
Hancock, NY 13783
607-467-2700

Active Homes Corporation
7938 South Van Dyke
Marlette, MI 48453
517-635-3532

Bristye Inc.
P.O. Box 818
Mexico, MO 65265
314-581-6663

ALH Building Systems
U.S. 224 West
P.O. Box 288
Markle, IN 46770
219-758-2141

Carolina Builders Corporation
Panelized House Division
P.O. Box 58515
Raleigh, NC 27658
919-850-8270

American Ingenuity, Inc.
3500 Harlock Rd.
Melbourne, FL 32934
407-254-4220

Classic Post & Beam Homes
P.O. Box 546
York, ME 03909
207-363-8210

Armstrong Lumber Co., Inc.
2709 Auburn Way N.
Auburn, WA 98002
206-852-5555

The Conifer Group
3140 S.E. Hawthorne Blvd.
Portland, OR 97214
503-239-0015

Deck House, Inc.
930 Main St.
Acton, MA 01720
617-259-9450

Deltec Homes
150 Westside Dr.
Asheville, NC 28806
704-254-2353

Design Pacific
3215 Meadow Lane
Eugene, OR 97402
503-689-3443

Endure Products, Inc.
7500 N.W. 72nd. Ave.
Miami, FL 33166
305-885-9901

Fairfax Building Systems
651 Maddox Dr.
Culpeper, VA 22701
703-825-3924

Fischer Corporation
1843 N. Western Pkwy.
Louisville, KY 40203
502-778-5577

Forest Homes Systems Inc.
RD #1 Rt. 522,
Box 131K
Selinsgrove, PA 17870
717-374-0131

Gentry Homes, Ltd.
P.O. Box 295
Honolulu, HI 96809
808-671-6411

Harvest Homes, Inc.
1 Cole Rd.
Delanson, NY 12053
518-895-2341

Hearthstone, Inc.
1630 E. Hwy. 25/70
Dandridge, TN 37725
615-397-9425

Insulspan Inc.
Foam Products Corp.
Box 2217
Maryland Heights, MO 63043
314-739-8100

Korwall Industries, Inc.
326 North Bowen Rd.
Arlington, TX 76012
817-277-6741

Lincoln Logs Ltd.
Riverside Dr.
Chestertown, NY 12817
518-494-4777

Lindal Cedar Homes
Box 24426
Seattle, WA 98124
206-725-0900

New England Homes, Inc.
270 Ocean Rd.
Greenland, NH 03840
603-436-8830

Northern Counties Homes
Rt. 50 West
P.O. Box 97
Upperville, VA 22176
703-592-3232

Regional Building Systems Inc.
5560 Sterrett Place
Suite 200
Columbia, MD 21044
410-997-7200

Saco Homes
21 W. Timonium Rd.
Timonium, MD 21093
410-252-3030

Shelter Systems Ltd.
633 Stone Chapel Rd.
Westminster, MD 21157
410-876-3900

Timberpeg
P.O. Box 474
West Lebanon, NH 03784
603-298-8820

United Building Systems
351 United Ct.
Lexington, KY 40509
606-263-5004

Wausau Homes, Inc.
P.O. Box 8005

Wausau, WI 54402
715-359-7272

Westchester Modular Homes
30 Reagans Mill Rd.
Wingdale, NY 12594
914-832-9400

Winter Panel Corporation
RR 5, Box 168B
Brattleboro, VT 05301
802-254-3435

Woodland Homes, Inc.
P.O. Box 202
Lee, MA 02138
413-623-5739

Woodmaster Foundation Inc.
P.O. Box 66
845 Dexter St.
Prescott, WI 54021
715-262-3655

Yankee Barn Homes, Inc.
HCR 63, Box 2
Grantham, NH 03753
603-863-4545

Other Panelized Home Manufacturers

American Standard Building Systems, Inc.
700 Commerce Ct.,
P.O. Box 4908
Martinsville, VA 24115
703-638-3991

American Timber Homes, Inc.
P.O. Box 496
Escanaba, MI 49829
906-786-4550

Amwood Building Components
Highway 30 W.
Toledo, IA 52342
515-484-5166

Amwood Homes
2833 Milton Ave.
Janesville, WI 53545
608-756-2989

Barden Homes
26 Copeland Ave.
Box 210
Homer, NY 13077
607-749-2641

Berkshire Construction Co., Inc.
P.O. Box 215
Falls Village, CT 06031
203-824-5476

Blue Ridge Homes
10620 Woodsboro Pike
Woodsboro, MD 21798
301-898-3200

Cedarmark Homes
P.O. Box 4109
Bellevue, WA 98009
206-454-3966

Citation Homes
1100 Lake St., Drawer AF
Spirit Lake, IA 51360
712-336-2156

Coastal Structures, Inc.*
P.O. Box 6490
Scarborough, ME 04070-6490
207-828-3919

Custom Made Homes
P.O. Box 1444,
416 S. Robinson St.
Bloomington, IL 61701
309-828-6261

Davidson Industries, Inc.
2110 E. Southport
Southport, IN 46227
317-787-3211

Denlinger, Inc.
P.O. Box 369
Paradise, PA 17562
717-768-8244

Endure Products, Inc.
7500 NW 72nd Ave.
Miami, FL 33166
305-885-9901

Enercept Building Systems, Inc.
3100 9th Ave. S.E.
Watertown, SD 57201
605-882-2222

Fullerton Building Systems, Inc.
P.O. Box 308
Worthington, MN 56187
507-376-3128

Forest Homes Systems, Inc.
Rt. 522, RD 1, Box 131K
Selinsgrove, PA 17870
717-374-0131

Gentry Homes, Ltd.
94-539 Puahi St.
Waipahu, HI 96797
808-671-6411

Hilton Lifetime Homes
33 Glenola Dr.
Box 567,
Leola, PA 17540
717-656-4181

Landmark Structures, Inc.
P.O. Box 405
Altamont, IL 62411
618-483-3131

Lincoln Homes Co.
P.O. Box 430
Smithfield, OH 43948
614-266-6440

Logangate Homes, Inc.
P.O. Box 1855
Youngstown, OH 44501
216-744-1100

Miron Truss and Component Corp.
P.O. Box 1598
Kingston, NY 12401
914-336-6000

NE Homes
270 Ocean Rd.
Greenland, NH 03840
603-431-6604

Pacific Components, Inc.
1227 S. Weller St.
Seattle, WA 98144
206-323-2700

Pacific Modern Homes, Inc.
P.O. Box 670
Elk Grove, CA 95759
916-423-3150

Pageant Homes, Inc.
4000 E. Holt Rd.
Holt, MI 48842
517-694-0434

Permabilt Homes
330 S. Kalamazoo Ave.
Marshall, MI 49068
616-781-2887

Regal Industries, Inc.
P.O. Box 509
Hope Mills, NC 28348
910-425-8162

Ronning Homes/Home Manufacturing & Supply Co.
4401 E. 6th Street
Sioux Falls, SD 57103
605-336-0730

Ryan Homes, Inc.
A division of NVR, Inc.,
100 Ryan Court
Pittsburgh, PA 15205
412-276-8000

Rycenga Homes, Inc.
17127 Hickory St.
Spring Lake, MI 49456-0534
616-842-8040

Shelter Systems, Ltd.
633 Stone Chapel Rd.
Westminster, MD 21157
410-876-3900

St. Mary's Precision Homes, Inc.
P.O. Box 597
St. Marys, PA 15857
814-834-4816

Stimpert Enterprises, Inc.
P.O. Box 427
Sleepy Eye, MN 56085
507-794-3491

Topsider Homes
P.O. Box 1490
Clemmons, NC 27012
910-766-9300

True Value Homes
2150 E. University
Tempe, AZ 85281
602-894-5388

Unified Corporation
4844 Shannon Hill Rd.
Columbia, VA 23036
804-457-3622

Wick Homes
400 Walter Rd.

Mazomanie, WI 53560
608-795-2261

Winchester Homes, Inc.
1321 Western Ave.
Baltimore, MD 21230
410-244-8112

Windsor Homes, Inc.
301 S. Stoughton Rd.
Madison, WI 53714
608-241-2185

Precut Houses

As the word suggests, a *precut* house package has the lumber for a house structure precut, measured, coded, etc., so that it can be easily nailed together to form a finished house. Some parts of the house, such as the interior partitions and kitchen and bath cabinets, may or may not be supplied with the package, depending on the manufacturer. In many cases, the heating, plumbing and wiring must be provided and installed locally by the buyer or hired contractors.

People who build their own houses often choose a precut house because it offers the greatest opportunity to save money with do-it-yourself construction labor. But, as noted in Chapter 14, the labor savings are not as great as some people believe. In all, the labor accounts for only about one-third of the construction cost of a typical house, excluding land, and about 16 percent of the total value or sales price of a new house, including land.

Still, the precut house offers other advantages and savings, such as special style and design features and no-down-payment financing for do-it-yourselfers. Also, precut home manufacturers will generally ship their packages long distances. Like the makers of panelized houses, most precut home manufacturers will also make houses to a customer's plans and specifications. Although no Precut Building Systems Council as yet exists, the manufacturers with asterisks are members of the Building Systems Council.

Adirondack Alternate Energy Co.
County Rt. 4
Edinberg, NY 12134
518-863-4338

Cedar Forest Products Co.
107 W. Colden St.
P.O. Box 98
Polo, IL 61064
815-946-3994

First Colony Homes, Inc.
P.O. Box 224
Calverton, VA 22016
703-788-4222

Fox-Maple Post & Beam
Snowville Rd., P.O. Box 249
West Brownfield, ME 04010
207-935-3720

Habitat/American Barn Corp.
21 Elm Street
South Deerfield, MA 01373
413-665-3563

Homes-You-Finish, Inc.
Builders of Martin Homes
and Renovators
6901 W. Shakopee
Bloomington, MN 55438
612-941-6101

International Homes of Cedar, Inc.
P.O. Box 886
Woodinville, WA 98072
206-668-8511

Lindal Cedar Homes*
4300 S. 104th Pl.

Seattle, WA 98178
206-725-0900

Logangate Homes, Inc.
P.O. Box 1855
Youngstown, OH 44501
216-744-1100

Martin Homes, Inc.
2600 Wayzata Blvd.
Minneapolis, MN 55405
612-374-1280

Miles Homes Services
4700 Nathan Ln.
Minneapolis, MN 55440
612-553-8300

Northern Counties, Inc.*
Rt. 50 West, P.O. Box 97
Upperville, VA 22176
703-592-3232

Precut International Homes
P.O. Box 886
Woodinville, WA 98072
206-668-8511

Shelter Kit, Inc.
P.O. Box 1, 22 Mill St.
Tilton, NH 03276
603-286-7611

Timberpeg East, Inc.*
Box 1500
Claremont, NH 03743
603-542-7762

Topsider Homes
P.O. Box 1490
Clemmons, NC 27012
910-766-9300

Log Houses

Nearly all log houses from manufacturers are sold as precut house packages, though the size and content of the packages vary from maker to maker. Most provide all the precut logs for the outside walls, but from there on you must check on what additional materials are needed to complete the house and whether the maker provides them.

Pay close attention to the kind of wood used for the logs, such as pine, fir, poplar, spruce or cedar. The type of wood selected affects the look, maintenance and durability of the house, as well as cost.

Like other home manufacturers, most log-home makers offer standard plans that they will modify for buyers. Most will also make log-house kits according to buyers' plans. Many also sell to customers for do-it-yourself completion or build a finished house, though the latter may depend on delivery location. Cedar is the most durable as well as the costliest, as mentioned in Chapter 7. Another important consideration is that, according to the Log Homes Council, some companies grade logs under an approved grading system. Paying extra for a house built with graded logs generally can mean a better built house, since your structure should stand up better over the years. It can be good insurance for many homebuyers, depending on such variables as the kind of wood logs used and the particular climate. An asterisk by the name of the manufacturer indicates that it offers graded logs.

Members of the Log Homes Council

Alta Industries, Ltd.
Route 30,
Box 88
Halcottsville, NY 12438
914-586-3336

Appalachian Log Homes, Inc.*
11312 Station West Drive
Knoxville, TN 37922
615-966-6440

Appalachian Log Structures, Inc.*
I-77, Exit 132, Rt. 21S
P.O. Box 614
Ripley, WV 25271
304-372-6410

Asperline*
RD #1, Box 240, Rt. 150
Lock Haven, PA 17745
717-748-1880

Beaver Mountain Log Homes, Inc.
RD 1, Box 32
Hancock, NY 13783
607-467-2700

B K Cypress Log Homes, Inc.
P.O. Box 191
Bronson, FL 32621
904-486-2470

Brentwood Log Homes
427 River Rock Blvd.
Murfreesboro, TN 37129
615-895-0720

Garland Homes by Bitterroot Precut*
2172 Hwy 93 North
P.O. Box 12
Victor, MT 59875
406-642-3095

Gastineau Log Homes, Inc.*
Old Highway 54, Route 2
Box 248
New Bloomfield, MO 65063
314-896-5122

Hearthstone, Inc.*
1630 E. Hwy. 25/70
Dandridge, TN 37725
615-397-9425

Heritage Log Homes, Inc.*
P.O. Box 610
Gatlinburg, TN 37738
615-436-9331

Hiawatha Log Homes, Inc.*
M-28 East, P.O. Box 8
Munising, MI 49862
906-387-4121

Honest Abe Log Homes, Inc.*
Route 1, Box 84
Moss, TN 38575
615-258-3648

Jim Barna Log Systems*
2679 N. Alberta St.
P.O. Box 1011
Oneida, TN 37841
615-569-8559

Kuhns Bros. Log Homes*
RD #2, Box 406A
Lewisburg, PA 17837
717-568-1422

Lincoln Logs Ltd.*
Riverside Drive
Chestertown, NY 12817
518-494-4777

Lindal Cedar Homes, Justus Div.*
Box 24426
Seattle, WA 98124
206-725-0900

Log Cabin Homes, Ltd.*
P.O. Drawer 1457
410 N. Pearl St.
Rocky Mount, NC 27802
919-977-7785

Log Structures of the South
P.O. Box 470009
Lake Monroe, FL 32747
407-321-5647

Lok-N-Logs, Inc.
P.O. Box 677, Rt. 12 South
Sherburne, NY 13460
607-674-4447

Maple Island Log Homes, Inc.
2387 Bayne Rd.
Twin Lake, MI 49457
616-821-2151

Mountain Log Home Co.
13080 Hwys 32 & 64
P.O. Box 0069
Mountain, WI 54149
715-276-3003

Natural Building Systems, Inc.*
Crockett Log & Timber Homes
P.O. Box 387
Keene, NH 03431
603-399-7725

Northeastern Log Homes, Inc.*
P.O. Box 46
Kenduskeag, ME 04450
207-884-7000

Northern Products Log Homes, Inc.
P.O. Box 616, Bomarc Road
Bangor, ME 04401
207-945-6413

Old Mill Log Homes
HC 89, Box 115-B
Pocono Summit, PA
18346-9711
717-839-1445

Pine Mountain Homes Ltd.
P.O. Box 549
Spearfish, SD 57783
605-642-7940

Pioneer Log Systems, Inc.*
P.O. Box 226
Kingston Springs, TN 37082
615-952-5647

Precision Craft Log Structures
711 East Broadway
Meridian, ID 83642
208-887-1020

Rapid River Rustic, Inc.
P.O. Box 8
9211 CO 511-22.5 RD
Rapid River, MI 49878
906-474-6404

Real Log Homes*
National Info. Center
P.O. Box 202
Hartland, VT 05048
800-REAL-LOG

Rocky Mountain Log Homes*
1883 Highway 93 South
Hamilton, MT 59840
406-363-5680

Satterwhite Log Homes*
Route 2, Box 256A
Longview, TX 75605
903-663-1729

Shawnee Log Homes, Inc.
8620 Roanoke Rd.
P.O. Box D
Elliston, VA 24087
703-268-2243

Southland Log Homes, Inc.*
P.O. Box 1668
Interstate 26 At Exit 101
Irmo, SC 29063
803-781-5100

Stonemill Log Homes*
7015 Stonemill Rd.
Knoxville, TN 37919
615-693-4833

Tennessee Log Buildings, Inc.*
P.O. Box 865
Athens, TN 37303
615-745-8993

Timber Log Homes*
639 Old Hartford Rd.
Colchester, CT 06415
203-537-2393

Town & Country Cedar Homes*
4772 US 131 South
Petoskey, MI 49770
616-347-4360

Ward Log Homes*
P.O. Box 72
39 Bangor St.

Houlton, ME 04730
207-532-6531

Wilderness Log Homes
P.O. Box 902
Plymouth, WI 53073
414-893-8416

Wisconsin Log Homes, Inc.
2390 Pamperin Rd.
P.O. Box 1107
Green Bay, WI 54307
414-434-3010

Woodland Homes, Inc.*
P.O. Box 202
Lee, MA 02138
413-623-5739

Yellowstone Log Homes*
280 N. Yellowstone Rd.
Rigby, ID 83442
208-745-8108

Other Log Home Manufacturers

Air-Lock Log Company, Inc.*
P.O. Box 2506
Las Vegas, NM 87701
505-425-8888

Amerlink Log Homes, Inc.*
P.O. Box 669
Battleboro, NC 27809
919-977-2545

Authentic Homes Corporation
Box 1288, 310 Grand Ave.
Laramie, WY 82070
307-742-3786

Bitterroot Precut, Inc.*
P.O. Box 12
Victor, MT 59875
406-642-3095

Cedar River Log Homes, Inc.
4244 West Saginaw Hwy.
Grand Ledge, MI 48837
517-694-7456

Colonial Structures, Inc.
1945 Union Cross Rd.
Winston-Salem, NC 27407
910-668-0111

Country Log Homes*
Route 7, Box 158
Ashley Falls, MA 01222
413-229-8084

Fireside Log Homes*
200 River Street
Ellijay, GA 30540
706-635-7373

Gold Hill Log Homes
P.O. Box 366
Gold Hill, NC 28071
704-279-7850

Greatwood Log Homes, Inc.
P.O. Box 707
Elkhart Lake, WI 53020
414-876-3378

Justus Log Homes
P.O. Box 24426
Seattle, WA 98124
206-725-0900

Lincoln Log Homes
6000 Lumber Lane
Kannapolis, NC 28083
704-932-6151

**The Original Lincoln Logs
Ltd.***
20063 Riverside Dr.
Chestertown, NY 12817
518-494-4777

Lodge Logs, Inc.*
3200 Gowen Road
Boise, ID 83705
208-336-2450

Lumber Enterprises*
75777 Gallatin Road
Gallatin Gateway, MT 59730
406-763-4411

Neville Log Homes*
2036 Highway 93N.
Victor, MT 59875
406-642-3091

New Hemstead Log Homes
P.O. Box 61
Creston, IA 50801
515-782-2890

Northeastern Log Homes, Inc.*
P.O. Box 126
Groton, VT 05046
800-992-6526

Northern Land & Lumber Co.
P.O. Box 291
Escanaba, MI 49829
906-786-4550

**Original Old Timer Log
Homes & Supplies, Inc.***
1901 Logue Rd.
Mt. Juliet, TN 37122
1-800-321-5647

The Rustics, Inc.
P.O. Box 949
Condon, MT 59826
406-754-2222

**Tussey Mountain Log Homes,
Inc.**
Box 53A, Rt. 1
Pittsfield, PA 16340
814-563-4972

Wholesale Log Homes, Inc.
P.O. Box 177
Hillsborough, NC 27278
919-732-9286

Yesteryear Log Homes
6000 Lumber Lane
Kinnapolis, NC 28083
704-932-0137

Resources for More Information about Log Homes Building Systems Builder (magazine)
14 West South St.
Corry, PA 16407
814-664-8624

Log Home Illustrated
P.O. Box 5740
Servierville, TN 87864
615-429-8335

Log Home Living (magazine)
4451 Brookfield Corporate Dr.
Suite 101
Chantilly, VA 22022
703-222-9411

Log Home Guide for Builders & Buyers (magazine)
164 Middle Creek Rd.
Cosby, TN 37722
615-487-2256

■ CANADIAN HOME MANUFACTURERS ■

In terms of construction, a wide variety of manufactured houses are made in Canada because of the huge spread of the country, from comparatively warm Nova Scotia in the east to the cold, rugged climate of the Yukon Territory in the west. A number of Canadian manufacturers sell their houses in the United States, if not worldwide, just as number of U.S. manufacturers sell north of our border or have subsidiaries in Canada. Before buying a house manufactured in the United States or Canada, make sure that it will conform to your local building codes. Here is a list of home manufacturer members of the Canadian Manufactured Housing Association (CMHA, 150 Laurier Ave. West, Ottawa, Ontario, Canada K1P 5J4; 613-563-3520). To find out information on the mobile homes manufacturers, you can write or call the Canadian Manufactured Housing Institute at the same address and phone number.

Modular Houses

Guildcrest Building Corporation
P.O. Box 10
20 Mill St.
Morewood, Ontario
Canada K0A 2R0
613-448-2349

Kent Homes
280 English Dr.
Moncton, New Brunswick
Canada E1E 3Y9
506-859-5650

Maisons Prince Homes
1150 Chemin Industriel
Bernieres, Quebec
Canada G7A 1B2
418-831-7000

Maple Leaf Homes, Inc.
P.O. Box 27
Fredericton, New Brunswick
Canada E3B 5B4
506-459-1335

MMH Prestige Homes, Inc.
P.O. Box 1580, Industrial Dr.

Sussex, New Brunswick
Canada E0E 1P0
506-433-4980

Nabco Housing, Inc.
686 RG. De La Riviere Est
Ste-Brigide Co.
Iberville, Quebec
Canada J0J 1X0
514-293-3125

Nor-Tec Design Group Ltd.
933 Coutts Way
Abbotsford, British Columbia
Canada V2S 4N2
604-859-2299

Quality Manufactured Homes Ltd.
R.R. #2, Kenilworth, Ontario
Canada N0G 2E0
519-323-2480

Royal Homes Limited
P.O. Box 370, 213 Arthur St.
Wingham, Ontario
Canada N0G 2W0
519-357-2606

Panelized and Preengineered Homes (similar to panelized houses in the United States)

Canadian Manufacturer's Wholesale Homes & Cottages
355 John St.
Thornhill, Ontario
Canada L3T 5W5
905-889-6937

Canadiana Homes
Box 65522
Dundas, Ontario
Canada L9H 6Y6
905-659-1622

Crawford Homes Ltd.
Box 53
Aldersyde, Alberta
Canada T0L 0A0
403-652-4011

Davey International
A Division of Davey Lumber
& Building Supplies Inc.
603 Tapleytown Rd.
Stoney Creek, Ontario
Canada L8J 3K8
905-662-6359

Descon Building Systems Ltd.
41 Empress Ave.
Ottawa, Ontario
Canada K1R 7E9
613-238-6777

Double S Prefab Homes Ltd.
14771C-64th Ave.
Surrey, British Columbia
Canada V3S 1X6
604-594-1777

Douglas Manufactured
Homes Ltd.
326 West 5th Ave.
Vancouver, British Columbia
Canada V5Y 1J5
604-874-2111

Habitations International
(Interhabs Ltd.)
Historic Properties
1869 Upper Water St.
Halifax, Nova Scotia
Canada B3J 1S9
902-422-2121

Halliday Homes
Highways 7 and 15,
PO Box 340
Carleton Place, Ontario
Canada K7C 3P4
613-257-3445

Igloo Building Supplies
Group
21421-111 Ave., N.W.
Edmonton, Alberta
Canada T5S 1Y1
403-447-3686

Imperial Homes
8629 Woodbine Ave.
Markham, Ontario
Canada L3R 4Y1
905-470-7772

Insul-Wall Limited
11 Mosher Dr.
Dartmouth, Nova Scotia
Canada B3B 1L8
902-468-5440

Lindal Cedar Homes Ltd.
10880 Dyke Rd.
Surrey, British Columbia
Canada V3V 7P4
604-574-3260

Linwood Homes Ltd.
Head Office/Sales/Factory
8250 River Rd.
Delta, British Columbia
Canada V4G 1B5
604-946-5421

Maple Leaf Forest Products Inc.
Manufacturing and Direct Sales
184 Highway 17 East
Echo Bay, Ontario
Canada P0S 1C0
705-248-2696

Modulex Inc.
3090 Hamel Blvd.
Quebec, Quebec
Canada G1P 2J1
418-681-0133

Nascor Incorporated
2820 Central Ave. N.E.
Calgary, Alberta
Canada T2A 7P5
403-248-9890

Nu-Fab Building Products Ltd.
701-45th Street West
Saskatoon, Saskatchewan
Canada S7L 5W5
306-244-7119

Pacific Homes
19486 60th Ave.
Surrey, British Columbia
Canada V3S 4N9
604-534-0656

Panelbeam Country Homes
Noramerica Building Systems Inc.
4160 19th Ave.
Markham, Ontario

Canada L6C 1M2
905-887-9616

Ratcliff Cottage Country Homes
PO Box 717
Gormley, Ontario
Canada L0H 1G0
905-888-1588

Scotian Homes
Enfield, Nova Scotia
Canada B0N 1N0
902-883-2266

Thermapan Industries
2514 Highway 20,
PO Box 479
Fonthill, Ontario
Canada L0S 1E0
416-892-2675

Valhalla Custom Homes Ltd.
355 John St.
Thornhill, Ontario
Canada L3T 5W5
905-889-0781

Viceroy Homes Ltd.
30 Melford Drive
Scarborough, Ontario
Canada M1B 1Z4
416-298-2200

Westwood Building Systems
5337-180th St.
Surrey, British Columbia
Canada V3S 4K5
604-574-0112

Log Homes (handcrafted)

Custom Log Homes Ltd.
3030-40th., S.E.
Salmon Arm, British Columbia
Canada V1E 4M3
604-832-3690

John Devries Log Homes
R.R. 3, Tweed
Ontario, Canada K0K 3J0
613-478-6830

Norse Log Homes, Ltd.
7411 North Island Hwy.,
Box 99
Lantzville, British Columbia
Canada V0R 2H0
604-390-3344

Original Log Homes
Box 1301,
100 Mile House, British
Columbia

Canada V0K 2E0
604-395-3868

Traditional Log Homes Ltd.
P.O. Box 2463
Salmon Arm, British Columbia
Canada V1E 4R4
604-832-8770

Ultimate Log Homes, Ltd.
1410 Alpha Lake Road
Whistler, British Columbia
Canada V0N 1B1
604-932-6000

Woodiwiss Log & Timber Systems Inc.
4936 4th Concession R.R. #2
Harrow, Ontario
Canada N0R 1G0
519-738-6251

Log Homes Profiled (precut homes profiled with a tongue and groove)

1867 Confederation Log Homes
R.R. #3
Bobcaygeon, Ontario
Canada K0M 1A0
705-738-5131

Algonquin Log Homes
R.R. #1
Norland, Ontario
Canada K0M 2L0
705-454-2311

Caledon Log Homes Ltd.
4 Holland Dr.
Bolton, Ontario
Canada L7E 1G1
905-857-2441

Canalog Wood Industries Ltd.
P.O. Box 905
740 Industrial Road No. 1
Cranbrook, British Columbia
Canada V1C 4J6
604-489-5200

Four Seasons Log Homes
Parry Sound Industrial Park
P.O. Box 631
Parry Sound, Ontario
Canada P2A 2Z1
705-342-5211

Grenville Log Homes
R.R. #2
Brockville, Ontario
Canada K6V 5T2
613-925-0508

Highland Homes Ltd.
P.O. Box 446, Garrett Dr.
Gander Industrial Park
Gander, Newfoundland
Canada A1V 1W8
709-651-3748

Laurentien Log Homes Ltd.
5636 Rt. 117, Dept. HBP
Val Morin, Quebec
Canada J0T 2R0
514-229-2933

Dovetail Log Homes
5500 Chemin Renaud
C.P. 55
Sainte-Agathe-Des-Monts,
Quebec
Canada J8C 3A1
819-326-6604

Hart & Son Industries Ltd.
Agents for Truecraft Log
Structures
P.O. Box 129
Whonnock, British Columbia
Canada V0M 1S0
604-462-9555

Maple Hill Log Homes
A Division of Maple Hill
Country Homes Inc.
P.O. Box 790
Mount Forest, Ontario
Canada N0G 2L0
519-323-3251

North Country Log Homes
Devon Mills Ltd.
P.O. Box 1180
Chapleau, Ontario
Canada P0M 1K0
705-864-1190

Original Log Cabins Ltd.
Box 239
Pine River, Manitoba
Canada R0L 1M0
204-263-5209

Riverbend Log Homes
Phoenix Wood Products Ltd.
P.O. Box 411
Nackawic, New Brunswick
Canada E0H 1P0
506-575-2255

**Quality Log Homes Ltd.
International**
1655 Townline Rd.
Abbotsford, British Columbia
Canada V2S 1M3
604-850-3655

True North Log Homes
P.O. Box 2169
Bracebridge, Ontario
Canada P1L 1W1
705-645-3096

Timber Frame Log Homes (made with natural solid wood timber in a post-and-beam framework and generally held together with hardwood pegs)

Acadia Post & Beam Inc.
P.O. Box 217
Port Williams, Nova Scotia
Canada B0P 1T0
902-542-2298

Canada Timberframe Co.
Box 2711
Huntsville, Ontario
Canada P0A 1K0
705-385-3441

Lukian Structures & Design Inc.
755 Route 329, P.O. Box 501
Morin Heights, Quebec
Canada J0R 1H0
514-226-5952

The Pat Wolfe Log Building & Timber Framing School
R.R. #3
Ashton, Ontario
Canada K0A 1B0
613-253-0631

Rocky Mountain Timberframes (Canada) Ltd.
P.O. Box 171
Okotoks, Alberta
Canada T0L 1T0
403-938-6793

Stavehouse
Box 132
Midhurst, Ontario
Canada L0L 1X0
705-721-1911

Thistlewood Timber Frame Homes
Thistlewood RD., R.R. #6
Markdale, Ontario
Canada N0C 1H0
519-986-3280

Timber Framers Consortium of Canada
R.R. #2
Orono, Ontario
Canada L0B 1M0
905-983-9354

Timbersmith Log Construction Ltd.
Hillsdale, Ontario
Canada L0L 1V0
705-835-3069

Upper Canada Post & Beam
Normerica Building Systems Inc.
4160 19th Ave.
Markham, Ontario
Canada L6C 1M2
905-887-9616

Index of Manufacturers

Index

184